JOSHUA
WE WILL SERVE
THE LORD

JOSHUA
WE WILL SERVE
THE LORD

JAMES MONTGOMERY BOICE

Fleming H. Revell
Old Tappan, New Jersey

All Scripture quotations in this book are from the Holy Bible, New International Version, copyright © 1973, 1978, 1984 International Bible Society. Used by permission of Zondervan Bible Publishers.

Quotations from *Joshua and the Flow of Biblical History* by Francis A. Schaeffer. © 1975 by L'Abri Fellowship, Switzerland, and used by permission of InterVarsity Press, P.O. Box 1400, Downers Grove, IL 60515.

Quotations reprinted with permission of Macmillan Publishing Company from YOUR GOD IS TOO SMALL by J. B. Phillips. Macmillian: New York, 1953.

Quotations from *Joshua and the Land of Promise* by F. B. Meyer (Ft. Washington, PA: Christian Literature Crusade, 1977 edition). Used by permission.

Library of Congress Cataloging-in-Publication Data

Boice, James Montgomery.
    Joshua: we will serve the Lord / James Montgomery Boice.
        p.   cm.
    Includes indexes.
    ISBN 0-8007-1615-9
    1. Joshua (Biblical figure)   2. Bible. O.T. Joshua—Commentaries. I. Title.
BS580.J7B65 1989
222'.2077—dc19   88-30210
                                                                                CIP

Copyright © 1989 by James Montgomery Boice
Published by the Fleming H. Revell Company
Old Tappan, New Jersey 07675
Printed in the United States of America

TO the Commander
of the army of the Lord

Contents

8   Contents

Preface

There are many influential people from past ages who, for one reason or another, have been largely overlooked by those who came after them. This would have been true of Joshua, Moses' successor, were it not for the Old Testament book that bears his name. Joshua is the story of this important military commander, the leader of the Jewish conquest of Canaan, and the inclusion of the book of Joshua in our Bible is undoubtedly God's way of calling attention to one who, apart from this inclusion, would have been completely overshadowed by his predecessor.

Yet the irony is this: In spite of having the book of Joshua in our Bible—the first book after the Pentateuch—many Christians are woefully ignorant of this man and of what was accomplished through him at this important stage of Israel's history.

Joshua was a soldier. He was a brilliant soldier, one of the most extraordinary military commanders of all time. But he was not an exciting person, as far as we can tell. He was probably just a bit of a plugger, a rather straightforward man who was chiefly concerned with carrying out his divine commission to the letter. He had no great sins and made very few mistakes. In short, he was not the kind of person who would make a good hero for a novel. Yet Joshua was eminently God's man. God told him at the very beginning of the conquest, ". . . Be careful to obey all the law my servant Moses gave you; do not turn from it to the right or to the left, that you may be successful wherever you go" (Joshua 1:7). This is exactly what Joshua did! And he was

successful! Joshua directed the Jewish conquest of Canaan for
seven long years, subduing all the great fortresses and cities of
the land. He led the people in a renewal of their covenant with
God. And at the very end, when he was at least ninety years old,
he challenged a new generation to be faithful.

> Now fear the Lord and serve him with all faithfulness. Throw
> away the gods your forefathers worshiped beyond the River
> and in Egypt, and serve the Lord. But if serving the Lord
> seems undesirable to you, then choose for yourselves this day
> whom you will serve, whether the gods your forefathers served
> beyond the River, or the gods of the Amorites, in whose land
> you are living. But as for me and my household, we will serve
> the LORD.
>
> Joshua 24:14, 15

This was a great challenge, but it was backed up by a lifetime
of faithful service to the Lord.

But the book of Joshua is important for things other than the
story of Joshua's life. Joshua is what Francis Schaeffer has called
a bridge book—something like the book of Acts. Acts is a bridge
between the gospels, which tell the story of Jesus, and the
epistles, which deal with the faith, life, and problems of the
church. Joshua is a bridge between the years of Israel's unsettled
wanderings in the desert and their settling down in the land.

This means that Joshua is also a book of continuities, and the
chief vehicle for these continuities is the Word of God. True,
there was not a great deal of the Bible in existence at this
time—just the books God had given the people through Moses—
the five books of the Pentateuch. But these were sufficient
revelation for the time. They told His chosen people what God
was like and what He expected of them. That is why Joshua was
instructed to obey everything they taught and not to turn from it
to the right or to the left.

As I have studied Joshua, I have become convinced that this is a message very much needed in our time. We have many professing Christians in our day: as many as 50 million in the United States alone, by some estimates. But we do not seem to have many Joshuas. We do not have many who, without trying to be novel or spectacular, determine to obey the law of God in every particular and then actually do obey it throughout a long lifetime of faithful service. Isn't it true that this is the chief reason for the church's weakness in our country at the present time? And isn't the chief reason for this failure our more basic failure to read, study, digest, and obey the Word of God?

We live in a literate age, but thousands of Christians are biblically illiterate.

Our age values leadership, but many merely bend with the wind of secularism or are swept along by the tide.

In publishing these studies of this important and fascinating book, I wish to express my deep appreciation to the congregation of Tenth Presbyterian Church, to whom I originally presented this material in the winter of 1985–1986, and to the congregation of The Above Bar Church in Southampton, England, to whom these studies were also presented (in a shortened version) the following summer. Each congregation assisted me with many helpful comments. I am especially thankful to those of the Philadelphia congregation for permitting me to spend much of my time in research and writing.

As usual, my faithful secretary and editorial assistant Caecilie M. Foelster checked this book and guided it through my side of its production. I am always very much indebted to her.

JOSHUA
WE WILL SERVE
THE LORD

Chapter One

Commissioning of a Soldier
Joshua 1:1–9

Be strong and courageous, because you will lead these people to inherit the land I swore to their forefathers to give them. Be strong and very courageous. Be careful to obey all the law my servant Moses gave you; do not turn from it to the right or to the left, that you may be successful wherever you go. Do not let this Book of the Law depart from your mouth; meditate on it day and night, so that you may be careful to do everything written in it. Then you will be prosperous and successful. Have I not commanded you? Be strong and courageous. Do not be terrified; do not be discouraged, for the LORD your God will be with you wherever you go.

Joshua 1:6–9

The book of Joshua belongs to that special class of biblical books that are named after their chief character. In fact, it is the first such book. None of the first five books of the Bible bears a proper name, though they deal with some of the greatest characters of history: Adam, Noah, Abraham, Joseph, Moses, and others. Joshua tells of the conquest of Canaan by the tribes of Israel under the command of Moses' successor, and it *is* called by his name. In this respect it belongs with such biblical books as Ruth, First and Second Samuel, Ezra, Nehemiah, Esther, and Job.

It is appropriate that this book is called Joshua, for although it deals with other matters, too, it certainly shows us the character and records the achievements of this extraordinary man. Joshua is often overlooked, as those who follow a particularly prominent individual often are. Who remembers the president after Abraham Lincoln? or the prime minister who followed Winston Churchill? As a category, successors are generally obscured by those who came before them. This happened to Joshua. In fact, this may be why the book is called by his name. Perhaps it is God's way of saying, "Have you considered my servant Joshua? He was extraordinary. He was faithful and hardworking. He was wholly given to My service. You should learn from his story."

I suppose it was while he was thinking along such lines that Phillip Keller wrote: "He [Joshua] has seldom been given the full credit he deserves as perhaps the greatest man of faith ever to set foot on the stage of human history. In fact, his entire brilliant career was a straightforward story of simply setting down one foot after another in quiet compliance with the commands of God."[1]

Joshua was not perfect, and the achievement of "setting one foot after another in quiet compliance with the commands of God" is hardly the way to command the attention and admiration of the world. Nevertheless, obedience is the key to victory in God's service, and Joshua is a noteworthy example of this point.

A Bridge in History

But Joshua is not only the story of a man. It is also the story of a conquest—the conquest of Canaan by the tribes Moses led out of Egypt. This means that it is a transition book: a transition from the patriarchal age, in which the nation of Israel was being called, formed, delivered, and trained, to the age of settled occupation of the land. It is not until Joshua that we have the fulfillment of the

1. W. Phillip Keller, *Joshua: Man of Fearless Faith* (Waco, Tex.: Word Books, 1983), p. 178.

promise originally made to Abraham: "To your offspring I will give this land" (Genesis 12:7). More than five hundred years had passed since that promise was given, but at last the time appointed by God rolled around and the people moved forward to possess their possessions.

Francis Schaeffer was impressed by this transitional element and called Joshua a bridge book.[2]

I have noticed three major approaches to Joshua in my survey of the basic commentaries. There is the liberal approach, in which the book is regarded chiefly as a *puzzle*. Rejecting its claims to be history, the liberal camp expends its effort trying to decide who actually wrote the book, when it was written, and what really happened. Operating along these lines, scholars can produce hundreds of pages of basically worthless speculation. Second, there is the conservative or fundamentalist approach, in which Joshua is regarded chiefly as an *allegory* of the Christian life. Conservatives do not doubt that Joshua is true history, but the history it contains has far less interest for them than the parallels they see between that ancient age and contemporary "spiritual" experience. The third approach, represented by Schaeffer, sees Joshua as a historical *bridge* in which the continuity of God's dealings with his people is emphasized.

Arthur W. Pink notices, I think with some justification, that this approach may well be suggested by the very first word of the Hebrew text, the Hebrew connective *vaw,* which is usually translated "and." I know, of course, that this is often merely a matter of Hebrew literary style. Many Hebrew sentences begin with *and.* But it is not just a casual thing.

Think it through. Genesis does not begin with *and.* This is to be expected, since it is the book of beginnings, and as a result there is nothing that goes before to which it may be linked. Genesis starts *beresheth bara Elohim* ("In the beginning God

2. Francis A. Schaeffer, *Joshua and the Flow of Biblical History* (Downers Grove, Ill.: InterVarsity Press, 1977), p. 9.

created''). The next book of the Bible does begin with *and,* and
so do Leviticus and Numbers. This indicates—we sense it
rightly—that these books belong together. Genesis, Exodus,
Leviticus, and Numbers form a unit and are the first natural
division of our Bible.

At first glance we might think that Deuteronomy, the fifth book
of the Bible, is a problem for our theory. It does not begin with
and, although it is the culminating book of the Pentateuch, the
capstone of the law. Yet, on reflection, we see why this is
reasonable. *Deuteronomy* literally means ''the second law.'' It is
a restatement of the law, a fact made most evident by the
repetition of the Ten Commandments, first given in Exodus 20,
and then repeated in Deuteronomy 5. As law, the first five books
go together. But as history, Deuteronomy marks a new beginning, and it is in line with this new beginning that the Book of
Joshua begins. From Joshua onward, each of the books begins
with *and,* thus linking each new book to the preceding book, until
one gets to 1 Chronicles. Thus the books from Deuteronomy to
the end of 2 Kings belong together and form the second major
historical division of our Bible.

This is also why Joshua is a bridge. In Deuteronomy, Moses is
the leader of the people. Joshua begins, ''After the death of
Moses . . .'' (Joshua 1:1). From this point on, Joshua, Moses'
aide, is the leader.

Deuteronomy contains instructions for what the people are to
do when the land is entered. Joshua quotes the Lord as saying,
''. . . Now then, you and all these people, get ready to cross the
Jordan River into the land I am about to give to them—to the
Israelites. I will give you every place where you set your foot, as
I promised Moses'' (Joshua 1:2, 3). The book of Joshua records
this conquest as well as the division of the land following the
conquest—all according to the promises and plan of God as set
down in specific detail in Deuteronomy.

So the first major point of Joshua is that God's purposes do not change. People change: All those who were twenty years and over who came out of Egypt with Moses died in the desert. It was a new generation that entered the land. Leaders change: Joshua replaced Moses. But God does not change. God is the same, and so are the purposes that he has established for his redeemed people.

The Written Word

The continuity between the patriarchal period and the period of Jewish settlement, based on the character and will of God, is focused on the written Word of God, which in this period was the Pentateuch, or first five books of our Bible. This is the second major point of Joshua. In Joshua 1:1–9, there are two paragraphs. The first (vv. 1–5) articulates the nature of the book as a bridge book: Moses is dead and Joshua is now to take over, knowing that as God was with Moses, so he would be with him (v. 5). The second paragraph (vv. 6–9) emphasizes the written Word of God that Joshua was to obey as he took his place in this succession.

In some ways these verses are the most important in the entire book, and it is because Joshua obeyed them that he is a great biblical figure.

> Be strong and courageous, because you will lead these people to inherit the land I swore to their forefathers to give them. Be strong and very courageous. Be careful to obey all the law my servant Moses gave you; do not turn from it to the right or to the left, that you may be successful wherever you go. Do not let this Book of the Law depart from your mouth; meditate on it day and night, so that you may be careful to do everything written in it. Then you will be prosperous and successful. Have I not commanded you? Be strong and courageous. Do not be terrified; do not be discouraged, for the LORD your God will be with you wherever you go.

These verses detail the special relationship Joshua was to have to the written law of Moses. But basic to that is the fact that there *was* a written law of Moses and that it was this, rather than some natural intuition or esoteric experience, that was to be Joshua's guide and source of blessing. Of all the many commentators on Joshua I know, Francis Schaeffer is the only one who emphasizes this adequately, showing that the *written* Word of God is the first and greatest of the many changeless factors in this history. Liberals do not emphasize this. They do not even believe it, for fundamental to the liberal approach is the assumption that the Old Testament books were written long after the events they describe and are intended to make the theological points of a later age rather than report the actual workings of God in history. According to most liberal scholarship, the Pentateuch was not even written at the time of the conquest, and Deuteronomy, the last of the five books, came very late in that long period of development.

The liberal understanding of the Pentateuch is encapsuled in what is called the JEPD theory. Each of those letters stands for a source or period in the Pentateuch's development. *J* stands for the "Jehovah source," the oldest portions of the law, which use the name Jehovah for God. *E* stands for the "Elohim source." This material used the name Elohim for God. Next came the *P* or priestly documents, and last of all came *D*. *D* stands for the compilations by the Deuteronomist or Deuteronomic school. Julius Wellhausen, who published this theory in 1878, dated the writing of the law in the fifth century B.C., after the Babylonian exile.

This is not the picture we have in Joshua. According to the very first paragraphs of this book, Joshua had the law of Moses. Moreover, the law of Moses already had the exalted status of a revelation from God.

This is something really extraordinary and terribly important. Here is the way Schaeffer puts it: "Joshua knew Moses, the writer of the Pentateuch, personally. Joshua knew his strengths and weaknesses as a man; he knew that Moses was a sinner, that Moses made mistakes, that Moses was just a man. Nonetheless, immediately after Moses' death Joshua accepted the Pentateuch as more than the writing of Moses. He accepted it as the writing of God. Two or three hundred years were not required for the book to become sacred. As far as Joshua was concerned the Pentateuch was the canon, and the canon was the Word of God. The biblical view of the growth and acceptance of the canon is as simple as this: When it was given, God's people understood what it was. Right away it had authority."[3]

This makes Joshua what I would call the first of the modern biblical books, in the sense that the situation it reflects is really parallel to our own. The Bible presents timeless truth; the God of Genesis, Exodus, Leviticus, Numbers, and Deuteronomy is the unchanging God who is also our God. But in these earlier books, the situation was different. God spoke to Abraham directly. God met with Moses on the mount. In Joshua, although Joshua is personally confronted by the "commander of the LORD's army" in chapter 5 and specific revelations are given to him for the conduct of the war through the high priest, the situation is basically different. Like ourselves, Joshua was to live by obedience to the written Word of God and not in hope of special revelations.

Even more, that written Word is what ties us to Joshua, just as it was what tied him to his illustrious predecessor, Moses. Indeed, the Bible is what ties us to God, for God has decreed that it is only through his Word that he will be made known.

The Commander's Commission

Important as it was to possess the Word of God in written form, as we also possess it, that was not enough to assure Joshua's

3. Ibid., p. 34.

success as Israel's new commander. He was not only to possess the Bible in a technical sense; he was to possess it personally. This is the heart of his commissioning by God. There are four parts to this commissioning.

Joshua was to know God's Word. That is, he was to read it and study it. Neither the word *know* or *study* is used in this section, but the other words presuppose them. If the law of Moses was to be Joshua's guide, as these verses clearly indicate it was, then Joshua would have to know what that law said. The first five books—his Bible—would not be laid up in the Ark of the Covenant as some revered relic to be looked at in awe from time to time but never touched. On the contrary, Joshua would have to get that book out on a regular basis or make a copy he could hold, read, and study as he sought to conform his thinking to the mind of God, the book's author.

This is a very important point. It is true that in this ancient period before Gutenberg or before scribes were able to make a reasonable number of copies of Moses' text, the people did not have their own Bibles. But this did not mean that the Bible was inaccessible to them or that they had an excuse for not knowing it. Joshua was to read the book. Later on, as at the ceremony conducted on Mount Ebal and Mount Gerizim, the law was to be read in its entirety in the hearing of all the people (*see* Deuteronomy 31:11–13).

I do not think this was a new idea to Joshua, either, for I cannot doubt that Joshua had picked up the importance of the law from Moses during the years of his association with him. If Moses had spent much of the preceding thirty-eight years working on these written documents (as he undoubtedly had), Joshua must have been a witness to that labor, have come to value that law, and know it to some extent. In other words, he must already have been a student of the Word, even before God commissioned him to his new responsibilities.

Do you seek leadership in Christian circles? Are you ambitious to serve God? Ambition like that is not bad; it is good. But if it is your ambition to serve God as Joshua did, you must prepare for it. The best possible way of preparing for it is to study and get to know God's Word.

Joshua was to talk about God's Word.   The text says, "Do not let this Book of the Law depart from your mouth . . ." (Joshua 1:8). Clearly, Joshua was to be conversing about the Bible in his normal day-by-day contacts with family, soldiers, friends, and others who were part of the nation.

How contrary this is to what passes for Christianity in many places today. Contemporary people are quite tolerant of religious folk in some ways. It is considered enlightened to respect others' practice of religion—as long as it is in its place (in church or synagogue on Sunday or Saturday) and does not affect the remainder of life. But let a follower of God begin to talk about God's Word at work or while out to dinner with friends or while golfing at the club, and suddenly tolerance begins to fade away. "This is not the place to talk about religion," the person is told. If the practice continues, the believer very likely finds himself or herself looking for new friends.

Joshua was to meditate on God's Word.   Meditation is a step beyond mere knowledge of the Scripture or mere talking about it. Meditation implies reasoning about the Word and deducing things from it. Meditation has application as a goal. Unfortunately, this is a discipline far too few Christians today know anything about. We live in an age of superficiality and spoon-feeding. Consequently, many of today's Christians think that all a person has to do to be successful in the Christian life is go to church, pay passing attention to the sermon, have a few Christian friends, and go on about their business as one would without these other elements. That is why Christians make so little difference in our society. They think like the world, and as a result, they act like the world. Their conduct and the conduct of pagans, apart from the grosser sins, is indistinguishable. What is missing? The missing element is deep, genuine, and persistent meditation on the Word of God. It is only as the Word of God gets into our minds and begins to become part of our normal, day-to-day reasoning and thinking that we begin to act differently and thereby make a difference.

Joshua was to obey God's Word in its entirety. The last element in this list of requirements is the most important. Not only was Joshua to know, speak about, and meditate on the law of Moses, he was also and chiefly to obey it. God said, ". . . Be careful to obey all the law my servant Moses gave you; do not turn from it to the right or to the left. . . . Be careful to do everything written in it . . .'' (Joshua 1:7, 8)

I think this is where much of our present-day Christianity breaks down. It is true that often we do not know the Word of God as we should. We do not speak of it as often as we ought or meditate on it persistently and profitably. But in this age of widespread literacy and numerous (though often superficial) biblically orientated churches, most of us know enough of the law of God to get on much better in the Christian life than we do. It is not that we do not know what is right; it is that we do not practice even what we know. We are not like the righteous man of Psalm 1, the man who "is like a tree planted by streams of water, which yields its fruit in season and whose leaf does not wither. Whatever he does prospers'' (v. 3). We are like the wicked whose works, even if (in the case of genuine believers) it is not they themselves, are "like chaff that the wind blows away'' (v. 4).

A Prosperous Man

Nearly everybody wants to be prosperous at what he or she is doing, yet most fail. What is the problem? The problem is that we do not follow the divine formula for success that was given to Joshua. According to the Bible, the secret of success is to know God's Word, speak about it, meditate on it, and then, above all, do it. In God's world there is no substitute for full obedience.

That was why Joshua was so successful. Joshua was a good soldier, but he was no more brilliant as a commander than countless others who have swept across the battle plains of world history. Joshua was a leader of men, but he was no more gifted at that than many others. Joshua's great secret was that he made it his job to know the law of God and do it. In Deuteronomy 27 there are instructions for how the law was to be read from Mount Ebal and Mount Gerizim after the people had entered and begun to possess the land. When Joshua got to that point in the unfolding of God's plan, he did exactly that—to the tiniest detail. Joshua did not try to second-guess or improve on God's instructions. Moreover, when he reached the end of his life this was still his overriding concern, for he instructed the people with very nearly the identical words God had originally given him: "Be very strong; be careful to obey all that is written in the Book of the Law of Moses, without turning aside to the right or to the left" (Joshua 23:6).

That is what we need today: not increasingly clever methods, still less increasingly clever people, but obedience informed and motivated by the living and abiding Word of God.

Chapter Two

In Command
Joshua 1:10–18

So Joshua ordered the officers of the people: "Go through the camp and tell the people, 'Get your supplies ready. Three days from now you will cross the Jordan here to go in and take possession of the land the LORD your God is giving you for your own.'"

Joshua 1:10, 11

The first chapter of Joshua contains two main parts: a section telling of the call and commissioning of Joshua and a section telling how Joshua assumed command of the nation and began to give instructions for entering the Promised Land. Joshua's assumption of command followed immediately upon his commissioning. The remarkable thing is that Joshua seems to have been afraid of this responsibility. I say this because the most repeated words in the chapter are those commanding him not to be afraid. God tells Joshua to be strong and courageous three times (vv. 6, 7, 9), then adds, "Do not be terrified; do not be discouraged . . ." (v. 9). At the end of the chapter, the people tell Joshua the same thing: ". . . Only be strong and courageous!" (v. 18). In spite of what must therefore have been a very acute sense of inadequacy, Joshua did indeed take charge. From the very first, he showed that he was the Lord's man for this hour.

Where did Joshua get this courage? How did he become a

leader? The answers to those questions are important as we look for Christian leaders today.

A Faithful Past

The first ingredient for good leadership is what F. B. Meyer, in his commentary on Joshua, calls a faithful past.[1] Joshua is the chief character of the book that bears his name, but his story does not begin in Joshua. It actually begins in Exodus and continues in the books of Numbers and Deuteronomy. In fact, Joshua appears twenty-seven times in these narratives, each time painting a picture of exemplary faithfulness.

The first battle.   The first appearance of Joshua in the Bible is in Exodus 17:8–16, which tells of the very first battle the tribes of Israel had after they had been led out of Egypt by Moses and crossed the desert to Rephidim. The battle was against the Amalekites, a semi-Semitic tribe that occupied the wide desert region between the southern borders of Palestine and Mount Sinai. Moses gave Joshua command of the Jewish troops in this battle.

This means that from the very first, Joshua was the leading soldier of Israel under the overall command of Moses. But the significant part of the story is the description of how the battle was actually won and the fact that this was to be recorded in the Book of the Law for Joshua's later remembrance and benefit. We are told that while Joshua was leading the armies of the Lord against the Amalekites, Moses went up on a hill overlooking the battlefield and raised his hands as a sign of God's blessing. As long as his hands were up, the Israelites were winning. But when he grew tired and lowered his hands, the Amalekites would begin

---

1. F. B. Meyer, *Joshua and the Land of Promise* (Fort Washington, Pa.: Christian Literature Crusade, 1977), pp. 19–21.

to defeat Israel. This became clear to Aaron and Hur, who were with Moses, so they had Moses sit on a large rock while they stood on either side of him and supported his arms. They did this until sunset, by which time the armies of the Amalekites were overcome. I cannot doubt that this was intended as a lesson for Joshua and that he learned it permanently and well. God could have given them the victory without Moses' raised arms, as he did on numerous other occasions. But in this, the first battle of Israel, Moses' raised arms were undoubtedly God's way of showing that the battle is not to the swift or to the mighty but that it is the Lord's. It is God who gives victory.

Joshua must have learned—and the story was recorded explicitly for his later benefit in this area (Exodus 17:14–16)—that although he would always have to do his best to be an outstanding general, he would succeed at that calling only to the extent that the Lord blessed him. He would have to seek that blessing.

Mount Sinai.   The second time we see Joshua is at Mount Sinai to which Moses was called by God to receive the law. When Moses went up the mountain, Joshua went with him, stopping partway. He stayed at his post on the mountain during the entire forty days that Moses was meeting with God: from Exodus 24:13, where he is first mentioned, to Exodus 32, when Moses came back down the mountain, joined Joshua, and moved to repress the rebellion that had erupted in the camp.

This must have been an exceedingly formative period in Joshua's life. Exodus 24:13, which mentions him specifically, is preceded by verses telling how Moses, Aaron, Nadab, Abihu, and the seventy elders of Israel (including Joshua) ". . . went up [into the mountain] and saw the God of Israel. Under his feet was something like a pavement made of sapphire, clear as the sky itself. But God did not raise his hand against these leaders of the Israelites; they saw God, and they ate and drank'' (Exodus

24:9–11). This surprising passage seems to describe a foretaste of something like what we call the great marriage supper of the Lamb. They saw God and actually ate and drank in his presence.

If this experience was anything like Isaiah's experience of seeing the Lord high and lifted up, which he describes in the sixth chapter of his prophecy, then Joshua and the others must have been shaken by this inescapable revelation of God's holiness. This would have increased Joshua's horror at the rampant sin later discovered in the camp when the Israelites indulged in their orgy around the golden calf. Joshua would have learned that sin is an abomination that cannot be tolerated among those who profess to be God's people.

The spies. The most revealing of these many references to Joshua in Exodus, Numbers, and Deuteronomy is the story of the sending of the twelve spies into the Promised Land in Numbers 13 and 14. As far as the land itself was concerned, the reports of the twelve spies agreed: It was a land flowing with milk and honey, a good land. They even brought back a huge cluster of grapes, pomegranates, and figs as proof of the land's fertility. But this is where the similarity ended. Ten of the twelve spies added,

> But the people who live there are powerful, and the cities are fortified and very large. We even saw descendants of Anak there. The Amalekites live in the Negev; the Hittites, Jebusites and Amorites live in the hill country; and the Canaanites live near the sea and along the Jordan. . . . We can't attack those people; they are stronger than we are. . . . The land we explored devours those living in it. All the people we saw there are of great size. We saw the Nephilim there (the descendants of Anak come from the Nephilim). We seemed like grasshoppers in our own eyes, and we looked the same to them.
>
> Numbers 13:28, 29, 31–33

Of all the spies, only two, Joshua and Caleb, thought differently. Caleb said, ''We should go up and take possession of the land, for we can certainly do it'' (Numbers 13:30).

The people of the land were the same, regardless of who was looking at them. The difference in the reports was due solely to whether the spies had their eyes on God, as was the case with Joshua and Caleb, or whether they had forgotten God, which was the case with the ten others. Some of the people of the land were giants; Caleb later asked to conquer some of them. But when the spies kept their eyes on God, the giants shrank to manageable proportions. The two spies were right to say, ''We can certainly do it.'' Later on in the story they add, ''The land we passed through and explored is exceedingly good. If the LORD is pleased with us, he will lead us into that land, a land flowing with milk and honey, and will give it to us''(Numbers 14:7, 8). On the other hand, when the ten forgot God, the giants seemed overwhelming and they appeared to be grasshoppers in their own eyes.

We know, of course, that the people of Israel decided to follow the majority report, forgetting God and despising his promise. For this they had to wander in the wilderness for the next thirty-eight years, until all who were over the age of twenty at this time died. This was a watershed moment, a tragic one. Nevertheless, it was a great moment for Caleb and Joshua. These two stood for God and his promises, and they were still operating this way nearly forty years later, when they again stood at the border of the land.

Joshua learned that the majority is not always right.

He learned that disbelief is fatal.

He learned that the only thing that matters in the long run is trusting and obeying God. He did obey; he was faithful to the very end.

Joshua's commissioning. The fourth important incident in

Joshua's career before the events of the book of Joshua was his human commissioning to be Moses' successor. The story is in Numbers 27:18–23, but echoes of the event occur many times afterward. Numbers tells us:

> So the LORD said to Moses, "Take Joshua son of Nun, a man in whom is the spirit, and lay your hand on him. Have him stand before Eleazar the priest and the entire assembly and commission him in their presence. Give him some of your authority so the whole Israelite community will obey him. He is to stand before Eleazar the priest, who will obtain decisions for him by inquiring of the Urim before the LORD. At his command he and the entire community of the Israelites will go out, and at his command they will come in."
> Moses did as the LORD commanded him. He took Joshua and had him stand before Eleazar the priest and the whole assembly. Then he laid his hands on him and commissioned him, as the LORD instructed through Moses.
>
> Numbers 27:18–23

Later the Lord charged Joshua, saying, "Be strong and courageous, for you will bring the Israelites into the land I promised them on oath, and I myself will be with you" (Deuteronomy 31:23).

I suppose that this commissioning took place some years before the death of Moses. So there was a period in which Joshua was appointed as Moses' successor but in which he was still only second in command—somewhat like David having been anointed king although Saul was on the throne. In some cases like this, a successor might behave himself badly. He might put on airs: "*I'm* to be Moses' successor." Or he might try to speed up the transition: "Don't listen to Moses; he's getting old. Listen to me." Joshua did none of these things. He continued to conduct himself modestly and loyally until, in God's own perfect timing, the transition actually took place. At the very end of Deuteronomy, in the same chapter that tells of the death of Moses, it is said of Joshua: "Joshua son of Nun was filled with the spirit of wisdom because Moses had laid his hands on him. So the Israelites listened to him and did what the LORD had commanded Moses" (Deuteronomy 34:9). F. B. Meyer wrote of Joshua concerning these years of preparation for leadership: "In his case, as always, the eternal rule held good, that faithfulness in a few things is the condition of rule over many things; and the loyalty of a servant is the stepping stone to the royalty of the throne."[2]

A Specific Call

The second ingredient that is necessary for strong Christian leadership is a call to it. There is an important sense in which we are all called to God's service in a general way. We are to be disciples of Jesus Christ and do good works (*see* Luke 9:23; Ephesians 2:10). But what I am referring to goes beyond this. It is a call to a specific work, and it gives a leader strength in the performance of that work, which he would not have if he had not received it. Joshua received this call in two ways: first, in his commissioning by Moses as recorded in Numbers 27 and, second, in God's detailed charge to him immediately before the conquest. It was because God had said, ". . . Get ready to cross the Jordan River into the land I am about to give to them—to the Israelites" (Joshua 1:2) that Joshua declared, . . . "Get your supplies ready. Three days from now you will cross the Jordan here to go in and take possession of the land the LORD your God is giving you for your own" (Joshua 1:11).

At the time this call came to him, Joshua was one of only two men in Israel who actually knew what lay ahead. Joshua and Caleb had entered Canaan with the original twelve spies thirty-eight years before, so Joshua knew the strength of the enemy. He

2. Ibid., p. 19.

had seen the walled cities. He had looked in awe at the giants. Humanly speaking, the majority report had been right: The people were invincible. If God were not with the Jews in this conquest, they would be routed and utterly destroyed.

But Joshua did not see things merely from a human point of view. He never worked out a military equation without God being the dominant factor in the equation. And when God called him, the possibility of conquering the land—which had always existed for him because with God all things are possible—now became a certainty, and he moved ahead vigorously. No person is as invincible as one who is certain God has called him or her to a task. No person is as bold as one who knows that God has already given him victory.

That specific call of God comes in different ways, and it is important to wait for it or seek it if it has not yet come. Many people have received a specific call of God while studying Scripture, recognizing that what they were reading had specific application to their lives. Some have received a specific call through circumstances, some through the work of God in others. Calvin was called to his great work in Geneva by William Farel, who threatened him with the judgment of God if he did not remain and help the Reformation. I received my call to the ministry in a subjective way when I was quite young. I knew that this is what God had called me to do. As I say, specific callings come to the people of God in different ways; but however they come, they are an important ingredient in leadership. The one who has been called to a work by God can give nothing else first priority.

An Objective Revelation

The third ingredient for strong Christian leadership is an objective revelation. The Bible is not merely to be possessed as one might possess another book, putting it on a shelf for decorative purposes or for reference. Rather, it is to be possessed internally as the words of that revelation are studied, spoken of, meditated upon, and obeyed. As we saw in the last study, nothing is so essential for success in God's service as knowing and building on the Bible.

What is important here is to recognize that this objective standard is necessary to control our subjective intimations about God's direction. If we are called to a specific work, it is inevitable that a measure of that call will be subjective. The Bible does not tell you specifically what you are to do in terms of a life vocation. If God calls you to be a diplomat, you will not find the Bible saying, "John Smith, I want you to work with the state department." God may call you to such a responsibility, but if he does, it will have to be subjectively, through a personal sense of call, through others (perhaps the church), or through circumstances.

But if that is the case, how is a person to be kept from merely subjective drifting? How are you to be protected from your subjective response to every conflicting gust of circumstance? The answer is, by knowing Scripture, laying it up in your heart so the categories of the Bible begin to form the pattern of your thinking and you begin to evaluate circumstances and the advice of others as Jesus himself would, if he were in your shoes.

I would suggest that the specific leading of God comes 99 percent of the time through Scripture and at best only 1 percent of the time through anything subjective. And even then, the subjective elements must be evaluated and corrected by Scripture. We see an example in Joshua 1. God told Joshua that the time had come for the people of Israel to possess the Promised Land. That might have suggested any number of specific plans to Joshua, plans that he might have validated on the basis of his personal call to be the people's leader. But although the call was a real call and part of Joshua's real success as a leader, Joshua nevertheless formed his plans in accordance with the written revelation.

In Numbers 32 and Deuteronomy 3:18–20, it was recorded that the two tribes of Reuben and Gad and the half tribe of Manasseh should be given the land east of the Jordan, but that they were to fight alongside the men of the other tribes until the Promised Land west of the Jordan was taken. Joshua remembered this writing and therefore made it part of his commands to these tribes from the beginning (*see* Joshua 1:13–15).

Faith in God

The final ingredient for effective Christian leadership is faith in God. It is needed as much today as it was in the time of Joshua.

In the first part of Joshua 1, there is a verse that is quoted in the New Testament and applied to us, and it concerns this very matter. In verse five God tells this great military commander, "I will never leave you or forsake you." (The same thing is said to Israel by Moses in Deuteronomy 31:6.) This text is quoted by the author of Hebrews in 13:5: "Never will I leave you; never will I forsake you," to which the writer then adds, "So we say with confidence, 'The Lord is my helper; I will not be afraid. What can man do to me?' " (v. 6). This is exactly what Joshua experienced and what he must have said to himself hundreds of times. God was for him. God had called him. He trusted God. Therefore, Joshua would lead the people into battle knowing they would be invincible as long as God continued on their side.

People follow a leader like that because to follow him is to follow God. This is why we find the chapter closing with the words: "Then they [the people] answered Joshua, 'Whatever you have commanded us we will do, and wherever you send us we will go. Just as we fully obeyed Moses, so we will obey you. Only may the Lord your God be with you as he was with Moses. Whoever rebels against your word and does not obey your words, whatever you may command them, will be put to death. Only be strong and courageous!' " (Joshua 1:16–18).

The people had not "fully obeyed" Moses, of course, and they would not fully obey Joshua. But that did not faze Joshua. He held on and did his duty to the very end.

Chapter Three

Rahab *Contra Mundum*
Joshua 2:1–24

> . . . *I know that the LORD has given this land to you and that a great fear of you has fallen on us, so that all who live in this country are melting in fear because of you. We have heard how the LORD dried up the water of the Red Sea for you when you came out of Egypt, and what you did to Sihon and Og, the two kings of the Amorites east of the Jordan, whom you completely destroyed. When we heard of it, our hearts sank and everyone's courage failed because of you, for the LORD your God is God in heaven above and on the earth below. Now then, please swear to me by the LORD that you will show kindness to my family, because I have shown kindness to you. Give me a sure sign that you will spare the lives of my father and mother, my brothers and sisters, and all who belong to them, and that you will save us from death.*
>
> Joshua 2:9–13

It would be a miracle as great as the crossing of the Jordan or the destruction of the walls of Jericho if Rahab, the Amorite harlot, knew Latin. Latin did not come to Palestine until the Roman occupation more than a thousand years after her time. Still, if she had known Latin, Rahab might have described her situation in Jericho at the time of the Jewish conquest as *Rahab contra mundum:* Rahab against the world.

Students of church history will be familiar with the words *contra mundum,* for this is the phrase used by the early church father Athanasius to describe his situation in the fourth century. Athanasius was born in Alexandria, Egypt, about A.D. 295, and he died in A.D. 373, full of years and honors. His life was not easy. These were the years of the great trinitarian controversies, and for much of this period, Athanasius was almost the sole defender of what we today recognize as orthodox Christianity. Essentially Athanasius defended the deity of Jesus, recognizing that the achievement of our salvation depends upon his being fully God. Athanasius was opposed on every hand. Emperors denounced him and frequently sent him into exile. He was exiled from his bishopric five times. The church turned against him. For decades it really was Athanasius against everyone. Yet his stance, though costly and painful, was for the sake of the true God, and God preserved him and gave him a total victory in the end.

This is how I think of Rahab and her stand against the world of Canaan. Indeed, in some ways her story is greater than that of Athanasius, for Rahab did not know of Jesus Christ. She had no Bible. No preacher ever proclaimed the truth of God to her. Yet Rahab learned about God and determined to follow him, whatever that decision might cost.

Rahab and the Spies

Rahab's story is set in the context of the story of the conquest of the land. It is intertwined with the story of Joshua sending two spies to Jericho, just as Moses had sent twelve spies to report on the land years before. It is interesting that Joshua sent *two* spies. Thirty-eight years earlier, when Moses dispatched the twelve Jewish infiltrators, only two returned with a faithful report to the effect that God would give the land to the people. Joshua was one of those, and his good friend Caleb was the other.

On this occasion Joshua did not want a repetition of the earlier disaster and so, perhaps symbolically, chose two men whom he undoubtedly selected carefully and from whom he expected a believing rather than an unbelieving report. Moreover, I think he had been directed by God in this action. The text does not say so directly, and some have supposed that Joshua was in error to send spies, saying he should simply have trusted the Lord and moved ahead. But God had told Moses to send the twelve spies earlier, in spite of the outcome (Numbers 13:1, 2), and it is reasonable to suppose that God had likewise instructed Joshua to do the same now. The spies were to go to Jericho and report on it in preparation for the attack that was to take place in just a few days.

If the spies were sent in obedience to the command of God, as we have every reason to believe, then we are probably also right to think that it was for the saving of Rahab and not merely for the bringing back of information that they were sent. Joshua did not need information about Jericho. What was needed were the arrangements by which Rahab and her family would be saved when Jericho was taken.

The situation here is similar to that in John 4:4, where we are told that Jesus "had to go through Samaria." It was not that the Samaritan road was the only road to Galilee; it was not. Usually, another way was taken. It was rather that God had one of his elect children residing in that city, and, as Jesus taught, not one of these elect sheep shall ever perish. Jesus entered Samaria to save the Samaritan woman. In the same way, the two spies were sent to Jericho to save Rahab. They did not know this, of course, any more than we know the outcome when we are sent on some errand for God. But in the divine view of things, this was the reason. God had been working in Rahab's heart, leading her to true faith, and now he was sending his messengers to confirm her faith and physically save her. It is interesting that the first character in this great book of Joshua, other than Joshua himself, is this woman and the first real story is her story.

Grace Abounding

Another way of saying this is to say that the first story in Joshua is a story of God's mercy rather than of his wrath. Joshua is a book of harsh conquest, and the premise for the particularly destructive nature of this conquest is that "the sin of the Amorites" had reached its full measure (*see* Genesis 15:16). That is, the people were ripe for judgment. All through Joshua, we see God commanding the Jews utterly to destroy the nations occupying the land, a judgment that has its closest parallel in the destruction of the people of the earth (except Noah and his family) at the time of the great flood. Yet even in this book of harsh and utter judgment, the very first story is about the salvation of the harlot of Jericho.

This is a story of great mercy, because Rahab had nothing going for her, humanly speaking. This is so striking that it is worth listing Rahab's liabilities.

She was a Gentile.   It is true that throughout the long history of the Jewish people, God demonstrated a marvelous tendency to reach out and save certain representative Gentiles. We think of Ruth the Moabitess or Naaman the Syrian. Still, as Jesus later said, ". . . Salvation is from the Jews" (John 4:22), and the only real advantages where true religion is concerned were in Judaism. Paul asked rhetorically, "What advantage, then, is there in being a Jew. . . ?" He answered, "Much in every way! First of all, they have been entrusted with the very words of God" (Romans 3:1, 2). ". . . Theirs is the adoption as sons; theirs the divine glory, the covenants, the receiving of the law, the temple worship and the promises. Theirs are the patriarchs, and from them is traced the human ancestry of Christ . . ." (Romans 9:4, 5). Not every one of these advantages was fully possessed by Israel at the time of the conquest, but most of them were, and—this is the point—it was *Israel* that possessed them. Rahab had none of these things. She was a Gentile and was, therefore, as Paul later told the Ephesians was their case, a foreigner ". . . to the covenants of the promise, without hope and without God in the world" (Ephesians 2:12).

She was an Amorite. The Amorites were only one of many peoples who occupied Canaan at this time. The standard list includes "the Kenites, Kenizzites, Kadmonites, Hittites, Perizzites, Rephaites, Amorites, Canaanites, Girgashites and Jebusites" (Genesis 15:19–21; *see* Numbers 13:29). But among these many peoples, who were now to be destroyed for their wickedness, the Amorites were singled out for particular condemnation for their sin. They were a corrupt, vile people, even sacrificing children in their depraved religious practices.

She was a prostitute. Here and there, there have been attempts to excuse Rahab from the full implication of this word, and some have suggested that since she had apparently come to believe in the true God prior to the visit of the spies, she must already have been reformed from her earlier sinful life. They argue that the spies would not have gone to the house of an immoral woman. Arthur W. Pink even argues from the presence of flax on the roof of her dwelling (Joshua 2:6) that she was engaged in a moral occupation—citing Proverbs 31, where the virtuous wife is said to work wool and flax with eager hands.[1]

Well, Rahab may well have been converted before the arrival of the two spies—I think her language does suggest that—but she is nevertheless identified as a prostitute, and it is undoubtedly because of her being one that the spies went to her. I am not suggesting that they went to her for immoral purposes. But where, pray tell, could two strangers go where they were least likely to be asked embarrassing questions? To go there was a stroke of genius. Moreover, when the king heard that the spies had gone to Rahab

1. Arthur W. Pink, *Gleanings in Joshua* (Chicago: Moody Press, 1964), p. 64.

and sent to have them brought out to him, he seemed to accept it as normal that men would visit Rahab and accepted her report that the men had left almost as quickly as they had gone in. No, there is no doubt that she was a prostitute, just as the Samaritan woman was also sexually immoral. It is merely another case of the great and inexplicable grace of God reaching out to save such a one.

Francis Schaeffer asks whether it is "fitting" that God should save such a person, and he answers quite correctly that "it is most fitting."[2] Rahab was no worse than we are, and yet God saves us. It is not the righteous but sinners whom Christ redeems.

Faith Comes by Hearing

In spite of this grim list of liabilities—a Gentile, an Amorite, and a prostitute—this pagan woman had at least one great thing going for her: She had heard about the God of Israel. As a result of that, she believed in the true God, for "faith comes from hearing the message . . ." (Romans 10:17).

This is where Rahab's great confession comes in:

> Before the spies lay down for the night, she went up on the roof and said to them, "I know that the LORD has given this land to you and that a great fear of you has fallen on us, so that all who live in this country are melting in fear because of you. We have heard how the LORD dried up the water of the Red Sea for you when you came out of Egypt, and what you did to Sihon and Og, the two kings of the Amorites east of the Jordan, whom you completely destroyed. When we heard of it, our hearts sank and everyone's courage failed because of you, for the LORD your God is God in heaven above and on the earth below."
>
> Joshua 2: 8–11

Undoubtedly, there was much about the faith and history of Israel that Rahab did not know. She had heard only of God's acts

2. Francis A. Schaeffer, *Joshua and the Flow of Biblical History* (Downers Grove, Ill.: InterVarsity Press, 1975), p. 81.

in delivering the Jews from Egypt and of the victory he had given them over the two Amorite nations east of the Jordan. But that was enough! She did not have the adoption, the covenants, the law, the worship, or the promises. But she had ears, and she heard what God did and believed on him as a result.

An interesting thought occurs to me here, because if we ask, "From whom had Rahab heard these tales of the God of Israel?" the answer is probably from the men who frequented her establishment. Her home would have been a place of great gossip as strangers from near and far reported their tales of foreign wonders.

"Have you heard what happened in Egypt?" one of them might have asked. He would have told how God had sent plagues on the Egyptians, plagues that turned the water of the Nile River to blood, brought flies and frogs upon the land, destroyed the cattle, and blotted out the sun. Last of all, he killed the firstborn.

"Did you hear what happened at the Red Sea?" another would continue. "The Jewish God parted the water so the people crossed over on dry land. And then he allowed the water to come back and drown the Egyptian soldiers who were following them."

"These people are still around," a third customer might say. "Not very long ago they defeated and killed Sihon and Og, the two Amorite kings east of the Jordan River."

I find this interesting, because although the Bible certainly does not excuse Rahab's prostitution, it was to some extent because she was a prostitute that Rahab received firsthand accounts of these things.

I said earlier that one thing going for Rahab was that she had heard of Israel's God, but I add that the wonderful (and saving) thing is that she had heard about God not only with her ears but with her heart. Here was an immoral, pagan woman who in the midst of the practice of her prostitution had heard about the true God of Israel and believed that the God she heard about was the true God. As long as that can happen—and it does happen—we can never despair about anybody and need not despair about ourselves.

By Faith . . . Rahab

When we say that Rahab heard with her heart as well as with her ears, we are saying that she believed in God or had faith. This is what she is praised for in the New Testament. Did you know that Rahab is held up as a model of faith two times in the New Testament? First, she appears in the list of the heroes and heroines of faith in Hebrews 11:31, where it is said of her, "By faith the prostitute Rahab, because she welcomed the spies, was not killed with those who were disobedient." Then the book of James says, ". . . Was not even Rahab the prostitute considered righteous for what she did when she gave lodging to the spies and sent them off in a different direction?" (James 2:25). Here is true faith, because it is faith in action.

We must marvel at what this woman did. It is true that she demonstrated her faith in God by welcoming and hiding the spies, who were God's representatives. This is what the texts in Hebrews and James say. But Rahab did more even than this.

Rahab put her life on the line.   She risked her own life and the lives of her family for the spies. Jericho was not a nice place. It was actually something of a military outpost, and we are not wrong to think that Rahab's life would not have been worth a wooden shekel if her deception had been discovered. If the messengers of the king had failed to accept her word that the spies had left before sundown and had entered her house and discovered the men on her roof, she would have immediately been dragged before the king and probably have been horribly tortured before being killed. Her family would probably have been taken and killed with her. Rahab must have known the risk she was taking, yet she risked everything on the basis of her spiritual discovery and new life.

Rahab repudiated her own past and people. This was a military situation, and Rahab knew, as the other residents of the city also knew, that when the Jews attacked the city, no quarter would be given. If the Jews succeeded in overrunning the city, everyone would be killed, just as the inhabitants of Canaan would kill the Jews if they had opportunity. Rahab was a resident of Jericho. Humanly speaking, she should have been loyal to her own city and people. Yet she repudiated her past for the sake of her new faith in the God of Israel.

Rahab identified with the Jewish people. She was not a Jew. But since she believed in the Jewish God, she now instinctively understood that her place was with this new people rather than with her own. In other words, in passing out of the kingdom of darkness into the kingdom of light she also passed out of the natural citizenship of Jericho to the citizenship of the children of God. In fact, since not even all Jews believed as genuinely as she did, she actually became more Jewish, spiritually speaking, than many of her new fellow citizens.

God accepted her new allegiance. We might imagine how, through mercy, God would receive her under the protection of the chosen nation and allow her to dwell in the midst of the favored people on a lower plane—something like the Gibeonites who were allowed to live among the Jews as ". . . woodcutters and water carriers for the community . . ." (Joshua 9:27). But that is not what happened. Though she was a Gentile, an Amorite, and a prostitute, she was immediately accepted as a full member of the favored nation. She married a Jew and became an ancestor of the Lord Jesus Christ. She married a man of the tribe of Judah named Salmon. Their son was Boaz, who married Ruth the Moabitess. Their son was Obed, who was the father of Jesse, who was the father of King David (*see* Matthew 1:5, 6). Isn't that tremendous? Rahab was not given a second-class salvation; from the very beginning, she received the whole thing. Her position was equal to that of any citizen of Israel, and in proof of that, she was brought into a noble line of the tribe of Judah and became an ancestor of our Lord.

The Scarlet Cord

Rahab's experience is parallel to that of everyone who comes to God through faith in Jesus Christ today. Joshua tells us that after Rahab had helped the spies and they had agreed to spare her and her family when the city was taken, they said, "This oath you made us swear will not be binding on us unless, when we enter the land, you have tied this scarlet cord in the window through which you let us down, and unless you have brought your father and mother, your brothers and all your family into your house" (Joshua 2:17, 18). Rahab agreed and tied the scarlet cord in her window. There is a tradition in the church, going all the way back to Clement of Rome and possibly earlier, that the scarlet cord represents the blood of Jesus Christ, and teachers have talked about the cord running all through the Bible, from Abel's sacrifice to Calvary.

I do not know if Rahab's scarlet cord specifically represented this, though there is a remarkable parallel between the cord that marked her house and the blood of the lambs spread on the doorposts and lintels of the Jewish homes in Egypt when the angel of death passed over the Jewish homes and families. But I do know that, whether or not that was intended to be explicit, the way of salvation has always been the same and the experience of those whom God saves is parallel.

For we are Rahab, if we truly understand her story. We were not at all part of the family of God or within the scope of what God is doing in a saving way in human history. What is worse, we were part of a corrupt, degenerate society in which we each had our own reprehensible sins. But God set his hand on us. He made his great saving acts in history known to us and then brought us into contact with his messengers and representatives. He called forth faith in us, faith by which through his grace we also laid our lives on the line. In a spiritual sense, we were called to repudiate our own people and identify with God's people. As a sign of that, the blood of Christ, like a scarlet cord, was spread over our homes and lives.

And now? Now we live in an alien land between the moment of our commitment of faith and the moment of the final judgment, which will be the time of our full deliverance. In this important interim we are to stand alone for God, as Rahab did: *Contra mundum!* We are to be God's people in opposition to the surrounding godless culture.

What if you have not done this? Then your state is the same as that of the citizens of Jericho. You look at the surrounding walls of your great secular city and say to yourself, "Surely I am safe here. The walls are strong. This city has stood for many thousands of years." But inside, your heart is failing you for fear, and you know that a day of certain reckoning and judgment is approaching. Why shouldn't you be like Rahab? She had nothing but a verbal report of the mighty acts of Jehovah, and even that was a selective, limited report. You have the law and the gospel, the law that condemns you for your sin and the gospel that shows you the solution to your sin through the death and outpoured blood of Jesus Christ. Why should you live any longer under God's just wrath and condemnation? Why shouldn't you believe on Christ, turn from your sinful past, and take your place with God's people?

Chapter Four

Journey Ended, Jordan Passed
Joshua 3:1–5:12

> ... As soon as the priests who carried the ark
> reached the Jordan and their feet touched the water's
> edge, the water from upstream stopped flowing. It piled
> up in a heap a great distance away, at a town called
> Adam in the vicinity of Zarethan, while the water flowing
> down to the Sea of Arabah (the Salt Sea) was completely
> cut off. So the people crossed over opposite Jericho. The
> priests who carried the ark of the covenant of the LORD
> stood firm on dry ground in the middle of the Jordan,
> while all Israel passed by until the whole nation had
> completed the crossing on dry ground.
>
> Joshua 3:15–17

You may have to think back quite a way in your life, perhaps
to when you were a child, but I am sure that you can remember
the excitement of a day for which you had waited a very long
time and which had at last arrived. Perhaps it was a special
birthday. Perhaps it was Christmas or the day you and your
family were starting off on a vacation. It may have been the birth
of your first child. For weeks, perhaps months, you waited. You
longed for the day. Then, suddenly, it was there.

It must have been a day like that on which the Israelites finally moved out of the desert across the Jordan River into Canaan. They had been waiting for this moment for a long, long time. Most had been born in the desert as part of that new generation that had replaced the one that had refused to trust God for the conquest years earlier. Joshua and Caleb had waited even longer. These men were about eighty years old, and they had been waiting for the conquest for most of their lives. Still, even this does not exhaust the extent of the Jewish anticipation of this moment. God had promised the conquest to Abraham more than five hundred years earlier (*see* Genesis 15:18–21). That promise had been repeated to the patriarchs for centuries. Properly considered, there had been half a millennium of fervent anticipation, and now the moment had come.

Joshua told the people, "Consecrate yourselves, for tomorrow the Lord will do amazing things among you" (Joshua 3:5).

A Total Narrative

In our Bible the story of the crossing of the Jordan River is spread out over three chapters, Joshua 3–5. But it is actually one story, and these chapters should be taken together for the story's full effect.

We see the unity of these chapters in several ways. In chapter 3 God tells Joshua, "Today I will begin to exalt you in the eyes of all Israel, so they may know that I am with you as I was with Moses" (v. 7). In chapter 4 that theme is repeated: "That day the Lord exalted Joshua in the sight of all Israel; and they revered him all the days of his life, just as they had revered Moses" (v. 14). Similarly, in chapter 3 Joshua tells the Israelites, "Now then, choose twelve men from the tribes of Israel, one from each tribe" (v. 12). We are not told here why they were to choose them, but in the next chapter the command is repeated and explained: "Choose twelve men from among the people, one from each tribe, and tell them to take up twelve stones from the middle of the Jordan . . .'' (Joshua 4:2, 3). The stones chosen by the twelve men were to be a memorial. All three chapters are linked by an emphasis on the covenant.

In these chapters there are three closely related events: (1) the crossing of the Jordan, (2) the erecting of a memorial to that crossing, and (3) the renewal of the covenant and the effecting of the covenant sign at Gilgal after the crossing of the Jordan but prior to the beginning of the conquest of the land.

The Ark of the Covenant

The most important thing about the crossing of the Jordan River, aside from the way it was crossed—in a manner exactly parallel to the crossing of the Red Sea at the time of the exodus from Egypt under Moses—is the prominence of the Ark of the Covenant in that crossing. It is even prominent in the telling of the story, since the ark is mentioned nine times in chapter 3, seven times in chapter 4, and is referred to indirectly four more times by the use of pronouns.

What is so important about the ark? The important thing is that it symbolized God's presence among the people.

The instructions for building the ark are found in Exodus 25, the first chapter in the Bible in which the ark is mentioned. From what is said there, we learn that the ark was not very big. It was a box about three feet, nine inches long and about two feet, three inches wide and high. It was covered with gold both inside and out and topped by a lid of pure gold, to which were attached two figures of cherubim or angels facing each other from either end of the cover. The wings of the cherubim were to stretch out and upward, nearly meeting directly above the cover. It was in that space above the lid of the ark and between the wings of the cherubim that God was symbolically understood to dwell. The ark was carried by means of poles placed through rings attached to the ark on each side. When the ark set out, carried by the priests, "Moses said, 'Rise up, O LORD! May your enemies be scattered; may your foes flee before you.' Whenever it came to rest, he said, 'Return, O LORD, to the countless thousands of Israel' " (Numbers 10:35, 36).

So here is the first important thing. When the people of Israel set out to cross the Jordan River at the beginning of their invasion of the Promised Land, *God himself went before them,* as must always be the case in any successful spiritual enterprise. When God was ready to lead before, they refused to follow. Then, they tried to advance even though God was not leading. The result in each case was a disaster. The only proper way to advance anywhere or at any time is by following God's lead. Only he can give victory.

Again, the significance of the Ark of the Covenant proceeding first into the Jordan is not merely to show that God must lead in any successful enterprise but that *it is the same God* who must lead and be followed. The God who led Joshua was the same God who led Moses and worked through him. The God of the conquest was the God of the exodus, and so on back to the time of Abraham and to creation. God is eternal; he is always the same in his eternal being.

The ark symbolized this. The ark symbolized God's sovereignty, power, or rule, and the point of the crossing of the Jordan led by the ark was that God was the same in his power on this occasion as he had been earlier when the people crossed the Red Sea under the leadership of Moses. The two miracles were intentionally parallel. God was no less sovereign on this occasion than he had been forty years earlier.

The ark symbolized God's holiness. Within the box or chest that was the ark itself were the stone tables of the law that had been given to Moses on Mount Sinai. The ark was the repository of the written expression of the moral character of God. It was a constant reminder that God was holy and that the breaking of his law was an affront to his nature and a rebellion against his rightful rule.

The ark also symbolized God's justice. It was not merely that it was in the presence of the ark that justice was meted out, though that was true. (When Aaron and Miriam challenged Moses' authority the three were called before the Tent of Meeting, which contained the ark, and Miriam was judged there [Numbers 12:1–15].) It was rather that the whole ark was a picture of God's judgment. Within was the law, which the people of Israel had broken. Above, between the wings of the cherubim, was the presence of the thrice holy God. As God looked down, he saw the broken law. Thus, the ark was a constant reminder of the need for the Judge of all the earth to do right. Judgment must follow sin.

But that was not all the ark symbolized. If it were all, it would be a terrible picture, indeed. The ark also symbolized God's mercy. The covering of the ark was called the "mercy seat" because it was there once a year, on the Day of Atonement, that the high priest sprinkled the blood that had been shed moments before for the sin of the people. The sin of the people was confessed over the head of the animal, the animal was killed in place of the people whose sin merited death ("the wages of sin is death . . ." [Romans 6:23]), and then the blood was carried into the holiest part of the tabernacle and was sprinkled on the mercy seat between the holy presence of God and the law the people had broken. In that way the ark testified to the principle of substitutionary atonement, to the fact that an innocent victim could die for those who were guilty. That principle can be traced back to the Garden of Eden, when God himself killed animals for Adam and Eve and clothed them with their skins. It culminates in the death of Jesus Christ on Calvary.

Thus, the ark pointed to the unchanging character of God. It taught that God is always the same in his sovereignty, holiness, justice, mercy, and other attributes.

Lest We Forget

The second event connected with the crossing of the Jordan River was the erection of a memorial of stones taken from the river. The text says:

> So Joshua called together the twelve men he had appointed from the Israelites, one from each tribe, and said to them, "Go over before the ark of the LORD your God into the middle of the Jordan. Each of you is to take up a stone on his shoulder, according to the number of the tribes of the Israelites, to serve as a sign among you. In the future, when your children ask you, 'What do these stones mean?' tell them that the flow of the Jordan was cut off before the ark of the covenant of the LORD. When it crossed the Jordan, the waters of the Jordan were cut off. These stones are to be a memorial to the people of Israel forever."
>
> Joshua 4:4–7

There is a technical problem that should strike anyone who carefully reads the account of the setting up of these stones. Clearly, the twelve men selected by Joshua were to take up twelve stones from the Jordan's riverbed and assemble them as a memorial on the west bank of the river. That is no problem. The difficulty comes from the fact that Joshua 4:9 *literally* says Joshua set up twelve stones in the middle of the Jordan at the spot where the priests who carried the Ark of the Covenant stood. This seems to suggest that there were actually two memorials: one made of stones taken from the middle of the Jordan and erected on the west bank at Gilgal and another of stones taken from the bank but erected in the Jordan. This is the way the older versions handle the passage, and as a result, most of the commentators (Meyer, Redpath, Schaeffer, Woudstra, and others) speak of *two* memorials.

Were there two memorials? There could have been, of course. But in my judgment, the New International Version is right in its translation in thinking that the words *had been* should be assumed in verse nine. If they are, the sentence would speak of setting up the twelve stones that *had been* in the Jordan where the priests *had* stood, rather than of setting up twelve additional stones in the river. In other words, there was only one memorial.

I think this is right for two reasons. First, the command of God to Joshua and through him to the people concerns only one memorial. Joshua could have decided to add a second one entirely on his own, of course, but this is not in keeping with his character or with God's original instructions to him to obey the Lord implicitly in all things and not to turn aside from God's law, either to the right or to the left. It is more like Joshua to obey the specific command of God and not add to it. Second, in telling the story, verse 9 seems to explain what happened to the stones taken from the Jordan, not how an additional collection of stones was set up. In this sequence we are told first that the twelve men bore the stones up out of the Jordan and put them down in the camp (v. 8). Then we are told that Joshua himself set them up as a memorial (v. 9). It is also significant that at the end of the chapter, when the stones are again mentioned, nothing is said of a second memorial in the Jordan. The verses speak only of the stones Joshua set up at Gilgal (v. 20).

Of course, whether there was one memorial or two, the point of the action was the same. The people needed a memorial because, like ourselves, they tended to forget the goodness and mighty acts of God on their behalf.

The story gives three specific reasons for this memorial. First, the generation that was entering the land to conquer it needed a memorial, because the road ahead would be hard and there would be times when they would become discouraged. The text refers to this generation when it says, ". . . Each of you is to take up a stone on his shoulder, according to the number of the tribes of the Israelites, to serve as a sign among you . . ." (Joshua 4:5, 6). By returning to Gilgal on a regular basis, as they did, since Gilgal was their base of operations, they would see the stones and be reminded of the power and faithfulness of the great God who was with them, leading them in their conquest.

Second, the generations to come would need this memorial, since children easily forget the faith and instructions of their

parents. This reason is emphasized in the story, both at the
beginning of chapter 4 and at the end.

> . . . In the future, when your children ask you, "What do
> these stones mean?" tell them that the flow of the Jordan was
> cut off before the ark of the covenant of the LORD. When it
> crossed the Jordan, the waters of the Jordan were cut off. These
> stones are to be a memorial to the people of Israel forever.
>
> Joshua 4:6, 7

> . . . In the future when your descendants ask their fathers,
> "What do these stones mean?" tell them, "Israel crossed the
> Jordan on dry ground." For the LORD your God dried up the
> Jordan before you until you had crossed over. The LORD your
> God did to the Jordan just what he had done to the Red Sea
> when he dried it up before us until we had crossed over.
>
> Joshua 4:21–23

Here, as well as elsewhere in the law, the people are reminded
to tell their children of God's mighty acts in past history so that
the children might not forget and might remain faithful to their
parents' God.

Third, the peoples of the earth needed the memorial as a
testimony to the existence and nature of the one true God. The
last verse of the chapter strikes this note: "He did this so that all
the peoples of the earth might know that the hand of the LORD is
powerful and so that you might always fear the LORD your God"
(v. 24). Francis Schaeffer says, "The stones were to tell the other
nations round about that this God is different. He really exists; he
is a living God, a God of real power who is immanent in the
world."[1]

---

1. Francis A. Schaeffer, *Joshua and the Flow of Biblical History* (Downers
Grove, Ill.: InterVarsity Press, 1975), p. 87.

Consecration

The third part of the story concerns the consecration of the people at Gilgal by reenactment of the covenant signs of circumcision and the Passover. This took place after the crossing of the river but prior to the assault on Jericho.

The interesting thing about this reaffirmation of the covenant is that it was the exact opposite of what worldly wisdom would advise. No doubt this was apparent to Joshua and the others, too, for it follows the report of the terror of the people living in the land: "When all the Amorite kings west of the Jordan and all the Canaanite kings along the seacoast heard how the LORD had dried up the Jordan before the Israelites until [they] had crossed over, their hearts sank and they no longer had the courage to face the Israelites" (Joshua 5:1). For the Canaanites, the events of the preceding days were a horror story. They had been terrified enough by seeing the Israelite hordes—some two million strong—spread out along the eastern bank of the Jordan. It was obvious that the Jews intended to invade the western lands. But the water was at flood stage. The people could not cross. There seemed to be time to get ready. Suddenly the waters ceased flowing, the people crossed over, and battle was imminent. The suddenness of the crossing terrified everyone.

Worldly wisdom would have called for an immediate attack while the people of the land were disheartened and before they could make last-minute preparations. Instead, God called for a three-day delay while Israel observed the two sacraments.

Moreover, the sacrament of circumcision totally disabled the army for a time. We know the effects of circumcision from Genesis 34. Dinah, the sister of Simeon and Levi, had been violated by Shechem, the son of the Shechemite king. When the Shechemites wanted to make the matter right and eventually intermarry with the Israelites, the sons of Jacob insisted that every male of the Gentile city would have to be circumcised first.

The Shechemites agreed to this demand, but it was only a ruse by Jacob's sons. The text tells us that "three days later, while all of them were still in pain . . . Simeon and Levi, Dinah's brothers, took their swords and attacked the unsuspecting city, killing every male" (Genesis 34:25). The Shechemites had been incapacitated by the rite, but it was precisely this rite that Joshua inflicted on his own troops at God's command.

On the one hand, this was the moment Israel should have attacked the Canaanite forces in Jericho. On the other hand, if the armies of Jericho had known of the circumcision of the Jewish army, they should have burst from their stronghold and attacked the weakened troops. Humanly speaking, the actions of the Jews were utter folly.

But the wisdom of God is not like human wisdom, and it was far more important that the hearts of the people be right with God than that they gain a momentary military advantage. That was what the ceremonies were all about. Circumcision was the mark of the covenant; it signified membership in the covenant people of Israel, just as baptism signifies membership in the covenant community of the church today. It was a divine seal on those whom God had chosen as his people, and it was a human response to the promises of God conveyed in that election. The Passover, the observance of which is described in verses ten to twelve, was a meal of remembrance, just as the Lord's Supper is a sacrament of remembrance for the church of Jesus Christ today. At Gilgal the people were to remember God's covenant, promises, and past acts of deliverance, in order that they might live as his people in the days that lay ahead.

We also need to learn that lesson. Americans are always anxious to rush ahead with some program, and the larger the effort and the faster it is executed, the better. We need to learn that this is not always God's way. What we do *is* important. But what we *are* is more important still. It is more important that God have our hearts and minds than our swords.

Chapter Five

The Commander's Commander
Joshua 5:13–15

> *Now when Joshua was near Jericho, he looked up and saw a man standing in front of him with a drawn sword in his hand. Joshua went up to him and asked, "Are you for us or for our enemies?"*
>
> *"Neither," he replied, "but as commander of the army of the Lord I have now come." Then Joshua fell facedown to the ground in reverence, and asked him, "What message does my Lord have for his servant?"*
>
> *The commander of the Lord's army replied, "Take off your sandals, for the place where you are standing is holy." And Joshua did so.*
>
> Joshua 5:13–15

These verses telling of Joshua's encounter with the leader of God's army are an unexpected vignette. The story of the crossing of the Jordan River and the consecration of the people and army proceeded with almost stately deliberation, spread out over the bulk of three chapters. Now suddenly, just when we are ready for an account of the assault on Jericho, we find three verses that tell how Joshua, walking near Jericho, suddenly came upon a figure who turned out to be a divine commander. Joshua did not recognize him at first. He is described only as a man with a drawn sword in his hand. But when he identified himself as commander of the army of the Lord, Joshua immediately fell down on his face and worshiped him. Can we doubt who this individual is? He is none less than Jehovah, appearing here perhaps in a pre-incarnate manifestation of the second person of the Trinity, the Lord Jesus Christ.

The Angel of the Lord

The story suggests this conclusion, of course, because the unannounced visitor would have instantly repelled Joshua's worship if he had been a mere man, just as Paul and Barnabas reacted with horror when the men and women of Lystra wanted to worship them as Zeus and Hermes (*see* Acts 14:8–20). But it is not only because of this story in Acts that we are prepared to identify the unannounced commander with God. We have been prepared for it by similar stories in the Old Testament.

The first such story is in Genesis 3, in God's appearance to Adam and Eve after the Fall. We are not told how God appeared to them, but the story does not suggest a theophany or other supernatural happening. We are told merely that "the man and his wife heard the sound of the Lord God as he was walking in the garden in the cool of the day . . ." (v. 8). This verse seems to suggest that God appeared to Adam and Eve in the likeness of another human being, or at least in a form capable of walking and talking to them.

A similar story involves the appearance of the three heavenly visitors to Abraham by the trees of Mamre. Some commentators say that the three visitors suggest the Trinity, and they may. The three seem to be regarded as one and even speak as one. On the other hand, it is more likely—in view of the way the story is told—that two of the three (the two who went on to Sodom and rescued Lot) were only angels and that the third was the second person of the Trinity, appearing in a form similar to that in which he had appeared to Adam and Eve.

We are alerted to this at the beginning of the story: "The LORD appeared to Abraham near the great trees of Mamre while he was sitting at the entrance to his tent in the heat of the day" (Genesis 18:1). In verse ten, one of the heavenly visitors speaks as God, to promise that Sarah would have a son by the same time next year. In verse thirteen we read, "Then the LORD said to Abraham. . . ." Further on in the story, as Abraham walks with the men for a distance to see them on their way, the text reads, "Then the LORD said, 'Shall I hide from Abraham what I am about to do?' " (v. 17). These and several other references suggest that Jesus anticipated his incarnation and was found in fashion as a man even before his later birth in Bethlehem.

The third story is of the man who wrestled with Jacob at the river Jabbok the night before Jacob's reunion with Esau. Genesis 32:24 called this figure "a man." Hosea 12:4, a later inspired commentary on the story, calls him "the angel." But even this does not say all that needs to be said, unless we recognize that this is "*the* angel of the Lord," that is, the special divine figure whom we have already seen on other occasions. This figure wrestled with Jacob to bring him to the point of submission, and then renamed him. Before, he had been Jacob, which means "supplanter" or, more colloquially, "cheat." Now, using the divine prerogative to remake and rename his creation, the angel called him Israel, which means "conquered by God."[1]

Presumably this is the same figure who appeared to Joshua to take command of his forces before the assault on Jericho.

God's Host

But even here there may be more than first appears on the surface. I have said that this divine figure came to take command

---

1. *See* my discussion of this change of name and its meaning in James Montgomery Boice, *Genesis: An Expositional Commentary,* vol. 2, *Genesis 12:1–36:43* (Grand Rapids: Zondervan Publishing House, 1986), pp. 334, 335.

of the Jewish armies, and that is certainly true. When Joshua asks what message the Lord has for him, we are to understand that this figure gave instructions for the ordering of the battle of Jericho, instructions which are carried out in the next chapter—even though that is not said explicitly. This figure undoubtedly assumed command of the armies of Israel from that moment forward and throughout the entire seven-year campaign in Canaan.

Yet "the army [or hosts] of the Lord" often means something quite different in Scripture. It refers to armies of angels. Thus, we are probably right to think of this figure as the commander of this greater army, which is standing behind Israel and assisting in her battles.

Here are two examples. First, in Genesis 32:1, 2 we are told that "the angels of God" met Jacob and that he named the place where he saw them Mahanaim, which means "two camps." These heavenly legions were God's hosts, and they were no doubt revealed to Jacob to encourage him and assure him that God would be his defense against attack. "Two camps" refers to Jacob's earthly camp and to the greater camp of the armies of angels.

The second example comes later in Israel's history, in a story involving Elisha the prophet. Ben-Hadad, the king of Syria, had been fighting the king of Israel. But every time he made plans to attack Israel, God revealed the plans to Elisha, Elisha told the king of Israel, and the Jewish armies escaped the trap laid for them. Naturally Ben-Hadad came to believe that there was a traitor in his high command. He demanded to know who the traitor was. The officers told him the truth, and as a result, he determined to capture Elisha. Elisha was at Dothan with his young servant, so Ben-Hadad marched out and surrounded the city by night.

The next morning, when the servant of Elisha awoke and went out to draw water, he saw that the ". . . army with horses and chariots had surrounded the city'' (2 Kings 6:15). He was greatly distressed. "Oh, my lord, what shall we do?" he asked Elisha. Elisha replied, "Don't be afraid. . . . Those who are with us are more than those who are with them" (v. 16). Then he prayed for God to open the young man's eyes, and when he did so, the servant ". . . looked and saw the hills full of horses and chariots of fire all around Elisha" (v. 17). These were God's angelic armies. They were powerful forces. In this engagement they struck the armies of the king of Syria with blindness so that Elisha was able to lead them into the fortified city of Samaria and capture them.

The Psalmist speaks of "the Lord of hosts," that is, of God as Lord of these heavenly legions, many times. Psalms 34:7 says, "The angel of the LORD encamps around those who fear him, and he delivers them."

In the New Testament the Lord Jesus Christ spoke of these hosts to Peter, saying, "Do you think I cannot call on my Father, and he will at once put at my disposal more than twelve legions of angels?" (Matthew 26:53).

In my judgment, this is what the commander's description of himself refers to, and as such it must have been a great comfort and encouragement to Joshua. Joshua must have been wondering how he was to proceed against Jericho. It was far too important a stronghold to bypass and leave at his rear. But on the other hand, it was well fortified. He could hardly afford a long siege while his inexperienced forces became progressively discouraged and the armies of the Canaanites gathered strength for battle. To have the Lord appear as commander of the heavenly legions must have lifted his spirits a good deal and assured him that the necessary force would be available when the assault on Jericho was finally made. And it was! It was the hosts of the Lord, rather than the armies of Israel, that demolished the walls of Jericho and permitted its overthrow.

For Us or Our Enemies?

There is something else about this story that interests me. It is the exchange between Joshua and the commander, in which Joshua asks, "Are you for us or for our enemies?" The Lord replies, "*Neither,* but as commander of the army of the Lord I have now come."

Isn't that fascinating? If we are right to understand this individual as the second person of the Trinity who has come with the armies of heaven to defend Joshua and secure the conquest of Jericho (as I believe we are), then why didn't he reply, "Yours. I am for you and Israel." Instead—although we know he *was* for Joshua and undoubtedly did assist in the battle against Jericho—the commander replied with a negation. "Neither," he said. That is, "I am neither for you nor for your enemies. I am here to command the Lord's armies." The point of the exchange seems to be that it was not for Joshua to claim the allegiance of God for his cause, however right it was, but rather for God to claim Joshua. The two would fight together, but Joshua would be following the commander of the armies of the Lord in his cause and battles rather than it being the other way around.

This is a most profound principle. Christians have a tendency to marshal God for their programs rather than simply follow him wherever he leads. As a result, the God they speak of seems to many outsiders to be quite partisan rather than the God of all men and women, which he truly is.

Years ago the English churchman and Bible translator J. B. Phillips wrote a book on inadequate conceptions of God. I have been much impressed with it and have had occasion to refer to it in various ways over the years. The first section of this book consists of chapters dealing with various weak gods: "Resident Policeman," "Parental Hangover," "Grand Old Man," and so on. One of these chapters, entitled "God-in-a-Box," is an analysis of the kind of partiality that I am talking about. It is a

discussion of the God of churchmen who view him largely as a
projection of their own denomination's concerns.

Phillips writes:

> All Christians, whatever their church, would of course
> instantly repudiate the idea that their god was a super-example
> of their own denomination, and it is not suggested that the
> worship is conscious. Nevertheless, beneath the conscious
> critical level of the mind it is perfectly possible for the
> Anglo-Catholic, for example, to conceive God as particularly
> pleased with Anglo-Catholicism, doubtful about Evangelical-
> ism, and frankly displeased by all forms of Nonconformity.
> The Roman Catholic who asserts positively that ordination in
> the Anglican Church is "invalid," and that no "grace" is
> receivable through the Anglican sacraments, is plainly wor-
> shipping a god who is a Roman Catholic, and who operates
> reluctantly, if at all, through non-Roman channels. The ultra-
> low churchman on the other hand must admit, if he is honest,
> that the god whom he worships disapproves most strongly of
> vestments, incense, and candles on the altar. The tragedy of
> these examples, which could be reproduced *ad nauseam* any
> day of the week, is not difference of opinion, which will
> probably be with us till the Day of Judgment, but the
> outrageous folly and damnable sin of trying to regard God as
> the Party Leader of a particular point of view.
>
> The thoughtful man outside the churches is not offended so
> much by the *differences* of denominations. To him, in his
> happy ignorance, these are merely the normal psychological
> variations of human taste and temperament being expressed in
> the religious sphere. What he cannot stomach is the exclusive
> claim made by each to be the "right one." His judgment is
> rightly empirical—did not Christ say, "By their fruits ye shall
> know them"? If he were to observe that the church which
> makes the boldest and most exclusive claim to be constituted
> and maintained according to Almighty God's own ideas was
> obviously producing the finest Christian character, obviously
> wielding the highest Christian influence, and obviously most
> filled by the living Spirit of God—he could perhaps forgive the
> exclusive claim. *But he finds nothing of the kind.* No denom-

ination has a monopoly of God's grace, and none has an exclusive recipe for producing Christian character. It is quite plain to the disinterested observer that the real God takes no notice whatever of the boxes; "the Spirit bloweth where it listeth" and is subject to no regulation of man.[2]

The title of Phillips's book is *Your God Is Too Small* and, of course, although Phillips is trying to expand our idea of God in his book, the title is the point of it all. Whether we are Anglicans with our high sensitivity to churchmanship and liturgics; Roman Catholics with our firm beliefs about apostolic succession; independents with our fear of being bound by forms or rituals; or even Presbyterians with our high regard for the theology of the Reformation, particularly in its Calvinistic forms, the God in our minds is always smaller than the true, living God, if only because our minds (however stretched by Scripture) are too small to fully conceive of or encompass him. We are always being surprised and stretched by God if we are actually dealing with God and not merely going through the mere outward forms of religious observance.

"Are you for us or for our enemies?" the devout believer asks.

Jesus replies, "*Neither,* but as commander of the army of the LORD I have now come."

A Touch of Heaven

The story ends with Joshua bowing before this commander. No doubt Joshua at first thought this unexpected individual to be what he appeared to be—a man and a soldier. But after he had identified himself, Joshua knew him to be very God of very God and so fell down and worshiped him. He asked, ". . . 'What message does my Lord have for his servant?' "

2. J. B. Phillips, *Your God Is Too Small* (New York: The Macmillan Company, 1967), pp. 38–40.

"The commander . . . replied, 'Take off your sandals, for the place where you are standing is holy.'. . .'' (Joshua 5:14, 15).

Haven't you known people who fit the description of Joshua after this encounter? I have been speaking of partisan believers who are so sure that God is like their particular denomination that they are unpleasantly intolerant of all other expressions of faith. We have known plenty of those. But I ask, haven't you also known people who are exactly the opposite? It isn't that they don't belong to a denomination or don't have strong beliefs about the true theology of the Bible, proper forms of church government, or Christian worship. They are anything but theological or denominational drifters. These people have strong beliefs, but they have something else, too. They have a larger, grander view of God, and as a result they are not primarily interested in whether others have dotted their particular theological *i*s or crossed their particular denominational *t*s. They are only interested in serving God, and expect him to lead others in his own way and according to his own timing.

What has made these people the kind of Christians they are? The answer is quite simple: They have actually been meeting with God, have bowed low before him, and have asked what he chooses to do with them. So they bear the touch of heaven and speak words which in some ways are the words of God.

We need people like that, and we need to follow them.

Chapter Six

Time to Shout
Joshua 6:1–27

When the trumpets sounded, the people shouted, and at the sound of the trumpet, when the people gave a loud shout, the wall collapsed; so every man charged straight in, and they took the city. They devoted the city to the Lord and destroyed with the sword every living thing in it—men and women, young and old, cattle, sheep and donkeys. ... . So the Lord was with Joshua, and his fame spread throughout the land.

Joshua 6:20, 21, 27

According to Lieutenant Colonel Faris Kirkland, former professor of military science at the University of Pennsylvania, the most exciting lecture he ever heard was on an ancient general's military tactics. The lecturer was a visitor to his class, not even a regular teacher. But he held his students spellbound as he described this man's military strategy: a sudden strike into the heart of the enemy's territory, thus dividing his forces, then campaigns to the south and north. He described techniques of psychological warfare, the elements of speed, surprise, and terror.

Who was this ancient military genius? The students suggested Alexander the Great, Napoleon, Julius Caesar, Attila the Hun. It was only at the end of the lecture, after all possible names had been exhausted, that the teacher revealed the identity of the one whose battles he was describing: Joshua.

The First Obstacle: Jericho

At one time the brilliant British Field Marshal Edmund H. Allenby must have studied this book, too, for Joshua's strategy was the one he adopted in his successful liberation of Palestine in World War I. Palestine is a hilly country, and the major passage through it is a connecting road that runs from south to north through the highest portions of the land. Joshua's strategy (and Allenby's) was to drive westward from the Jordan Valley to that high road, thus dividing the country. Then, when the enemy forces were divided, they would first destroy the opposition to the south and then the opposition to the north. This is the outline of the campaign described in Joshua 6–11.

Before the country could be divided, a wedge had to be driven from the Jordan River valley to the mountains. The first obstacle was at this point: Jericho. Jericho was a military fortress built to defend the eastern approach to the high country. It could not be bypassed; to bypass Jericho would mean leaving a large military force at one's rear. But, on the other hand, conquering Jericho was a dismaying challenge. Jericho's walls were high, its position advantageous. What was Joshua to do with an obstacle of these proportions?

If Joshua had held a council of war, it is not hard to imagine the advice he might have been given. One adviser might have argued that the way to take fortified cities is by siege ramps. An approach to the top of the walls must be constructed. (This was the way the Romans took fortified cities more than a thousand years later.) Another might have argued for starving Jericho's defenders into submission. "Seal up the city," he might have argued. "They cannot hold out forever. Eventually they will come to terms, open the city gates, and surrender."

The story shows that Joshua adopted none of these counsels; in fact, he did not even seek them. He was already in touch with one who was the true strategist and commander.

The true commander, whom we met at the end of chapter five, had a unique plan for this battle. He told Joshua:

> See, I have delivered Jericho into your hands, along with its king and its fighting men. March around the city once with all the armed men. Do this for six days. Have seven priests carry trumpets of rams' horns in front of the ark. On the seventh day, march around the city seven times, with the priests blowing the trumpets. When you hear them sound a long blast on the trumpets, have all the people give a loud shout; then the wall of the city will collapse and the people will go up, every man straight in.
>
> Joshua 6:2–5

From a human point of view, nothing could have been more useless, in spite of the obvious necessity of attacking this outpost. High walls do not fall to the noise of tramping feet. Cities are not won by trumpets.

Yet this is precisely what happened. The story tells how the people followed the commands of the Lord. Each day for six days they walked in silence around the watching city, and on the seventh day they repeated this apparently futile exercise seven times. No one spoke. The only noise was the sound of the rams' horns blown by the priests. Then, on the seventh circuit on the seventh day, when the city was entirely surrounded by the Jewish armies, Joshua commanded the people, "Shout! For the LORD has given you the city!" (v. 16). The people did shout! It was the time to shout! "When the trumpets sounded, the people shouted, and at the sound of the trumpet, when the people gave a loud shout, the wall collapsed; so every man charged straight in, and they took the city" (v. 20).

Jericho was destroyed in accordance with God's command to Joshua. Only Rahab and her family were spared because of her having saved the two spies.

The Path to Victory

I was in a meeting in which a pastor was reporting on the revivals that have been taking place in the South American country of Argentina. That country is wide open to the gospel, and tens of thousands of people are coming to faith in Christ regularly in large open-air meetings. What is so striking about this revival, as it was related to me, is the preparation that had been made for it as long as twenty years before. At that time, the leaders of the Argentinian church began to pray for revival and ask themselves what they should do to prepare for the blessing they were asking God to send. Where would they put the people they were asking to be converted? How would they disciple the anticipated additions to the church? Their plan was to train leaders for greatly expanded churches and to establish strong Christian homes in which counseling and discipling could be done.

I think of that report as I study the account of the Jews' conquest of Jericho, for one thing that is unmistakably clear is that there had been preparation before the shout of victory. Some of that preparation had started forty years earlier in the preparation of Joshua and Caleb and the soldiers that had been trained in the wilderness. More preparation had taken place after the Jordan River had been crossed. There was a reinstitution of the covenantal rite of circumcision and a new observance of the Passover. The hearts of the people had to be right before there could be a full outpouring of God's blessing.

But the preparation did not stop there. In fact, it continued right up to the very moment of the shout. Everything before that moment was preparation of the hearts of the people. The story stresses three steps.

Silence.   The first step in the preparation of the people for this climactic week was the command to keep silent. They were to be utterly quiet as they encircled the doomed city. Their lips were not to speak a word. The text says, "Joshua had commanded the people, 'Do not give a war cry, do not raise your voices, do not say a word until the day I tell you to shout. Then shout!' " (Joshua 6:10).

This must have been a difficult thing for the people to do. For one thing, there were several million people, and it is hard to imagine any large group of people moving anywhere without an increasingly noisy hum, then roar of voices. There were soldiers to get in line, children to keep track of, a route to be pointed out and taken. How this could be accomplished in silence I do not know, but this is what the people did. Moreover, the people would have had difficulty ignoring the taunts of the encircled citizens of Jericho. On the first day the Canaanites would probably have been quiet, too, watching to see what the encircling armies would do. It would have been bizarre: a silent attacking force watched by silent defenders. But silence would hardly have lasted beyond the second day. By then, the defenders would have begun to mock the Jewish soldiers: "What do you think you're doing, marching around our walls? Do you think we're so foolish as to have left a door open somewhere? Are you afraid to fight? Why don't you try to get in? We'll show you how a city should be defended. Cowards!" Under such circumstances, it would have been difficult for the Jewish people to have kept silent.

What do you think they were thinking about? I suspect they must have been thinking that there was no possibility of conquering Jericho unless God delivered it to them. Jericho's walls were high. The gates were shut. Each circling of the walls would have helped them realize that if there was to be a victory, it would have to be given to them by God.

Silence before God; this is a lesson we all need to learn. The Argentinian evangelist Luis Palau writes, "What a rare commodity! How difficult this is to achieve. If we're not speaking verbally, then there are a thousand mental voices inside our thoughts, each vying for the last word. Listen to God? How can

he possibly get a word in edgewise? This passage seems to be
saying, 'Hush. Don't talk so much. Be quiet before the Lord after
you've poured out your heart to him. Let God speak.' "[1]

F. B. Meyer calls "Silence!" the hardest of all commandments:

> That our voice should not be heard; that no word should
> proceed from our mouth; that we should utter our complaints to
> God alone—all this is foreign to our habits and taste. As death
> is the last enemy to be destroyed in the universe of God, so is
> the restraint of the tongue the last lesson learned by his
> children. We like to air our grievances; to talk over our
> ailments; to compare ourselves with others; and to discuss the
> likeliest remedies. We tell our friends our secrets under strict
> promises of confidence, to discover in bitter experience the
> truth of the Master's words, that what is told into the ear in
> closets will be proclaimed upon housetops.
>
> It is only the still heart that can reflect the heaven of God's
> overarching care, or detect the least whisper of his voice
> through its quiet atmosphere, or know his full grace and
> power.[2]

Obedience.   The second step in the preparation of the people
for the conquest of Jericho was obedience. Obedience is an
essential part of true faith, which is why, I suppose, the actions
of the people are cited in Hebrews as a demonstration of faith.
"*By faith* the walls of Jericho fell, after the people had marched
around them for seven days" (Hebrews 11:30, emphasis mine).

What is it that most honors God and which God most delights
to honor? Is it eloquent profession of faith? No. Many have called
Jesus "Lord, Lord" but have later fallen away and ceased to
serve him. Is it the exercise of great natural abilities or talents?
No. There are many who have had great abilities but have

---

1. Luis Palau, *The Moment to Shout* (Portland: Multnomah Press, 1977), pp.
113, 114.
2. F. B. Meyer, *Joshua and the Land of Promise* (Fort Washington, Pa.:
Christian Literature Crusade, 1977), p. 78.

squandered them on worthless ends, like the prodigal who squandered his father's money. Is it an attractive appearance or personality? No. Saul stood head and shoulders above his countrymen, a great physical specimen, but he finished his course badly. The true answer to the question is found in Samuel's words to Saul after he had sinned by failing to destroy the Amalekites completely, which God had told him to do. Saul pleaded that he had almost entirely destroyed them and that he had spared what he did spare only to make sacrifices. But Samuel declared,

> Does the LORD delight in burnt offerings and sacrifices
>   as much as in obeying the voice of the LORD?
> To obey is better than sacrifice,
>   and to heed is better than the fat of rams.
>
> 1 Samuel 15:22

That is the answer. The thing that most honors God and that God most delights to honor is obedience. Even Jesus was honored and given a name above every name because he was obedient: ". . . obedient to death—even death on a cross!" (Philippians 2:8).

Obedience to the very end.   The third step in the preparation of the Jewish people for victory was obedience to the very end. This is involved in the previous point, of course, because obedience that is not total is not real obedience; it is disobedience, as the story of Saul's failure to destroy the Amalekites shows. It is only necessary to highlight this as a separate point because of our frequent failure to continue on this path.

The conquest of Jericho emphasizes this achievement by the Jewish invaders. Careful reading of the story shows that Joshua did not tell the people how many times they were going to be required to circle the city or precisely what was going to happen at the end of their seven days' marching. The people were given their instructions one day at a time, and at the end of their assignment for that day, having encircled the walls, they were directed back to their camp. *And nothing happened!* They had obeyed Joshua, who had been obeying God. They had encircled the walls. But when they returned to camp, the walls were still standing, no one had surrendered, and the Jewish armies seemed to be no closer to the final conquest of Canaan than they had been the day before. So it was after the second day . . . and the third . . . and the fourth . . . and the fifth . . . and the sixth. . . . So it also was after six tours around the walls on day seven.

The situation reminds me of what must have happened after the Syrian general Naaman had been told by Elisha that he would be cured of his leprosy if he bathed in the Jordan River seven times. We know he did not like the idea because he protested about the inferiority of the Jordan River to the rivers of his own country. ". . . I thought that he would surely come out to me and stand and call on the name of the LORD his God, wave his hand over the spot and cure me of my leprosy. Are not Abana and Pharpar, the rivers of Damascus, better than any of the waters of Israel? Couldn't I wash in them and be cleansed'. . . ?" Naaman asked (2 Kings 5:11, 12).

It must have been a great trial to this proud general to wash in Jordan's muddy waters *seven* times, and I can imagine him objecting to his servant who, in this story, had more spiritual sense than Naaman had. After he had bathed once, Naaman would have protested: "Look, I bathed in the river, but I am just as I was before. Nothing happened."

"The prophet said you had to bathe seven times," the servant would have answered.

After the second immersion, the protest would have been the same. There was not even the slightest hint that the method was working. Not a single spot had cleared up. The only difference was that the general was wet and muddy. So on after the third washing and the fourth and the fifth and the sixth. "Nothing is happening," the angry Naaman would have declared.

"You've only dipped yourself in the water six times," the servant would have said. "The prophet said seven." It was only after the seventh washing, after total obedience to the very end, that ". . . his flesh was restored and became clean like that of a young boy" (2 Kings 5:14).

We need to learn the lesson the Jewish armies learned before Jericho and Naaman the Syrian learned in the muddy Jordan River. Not only is there no substitute for obedience to God, there is no substitute for obedience in all particulars—to the very end. And when God does not act as quickly as we think he should or in precisely the way we are convinced he should act, we are still not justified in pulling back or adopting an alternative procedure. Arthur W. Pink has written of this story, "Seeming failure did not warrant them in adopting *other* measures; they must adhere strictly to the divine directions unto the end."[3] It was only when the people had obeyed God faithfully that victory came and the walls tumbled.

Demolishing Strongholds

I close with two applications. First, if you are a Christian, you are a soldier in God's army and are engaged in a war where many enemy strongholds need to be conquered. We see them everywhere. There are fortresses of evil in our land, in the church and, we must confess, in ourselves. They are surrounded by high walls. The gates are sealed. They are manned by strong and experienced defenders. What are we to do against such ancient outposts of God's and our enemy? The anwer is that we are to assault them in the way God has told us to wage warfare: by prayer, by the Word

3. Arthur W. Pink, *Gleanings in Joshua* (Chicago: Moody Press, 1964), p. 165.

of God, and by our testimony. When we look at evil's forces we may think the ancient weapons of the church are inadequate, and we may be greatly tempted to abandon them and use the world's tools. This is a mistake. We need to listen to God and obey faithfully to the very end. When we do, then in God's own time, the walls of Satan's strongholds will tumble.

The apostle Paul wrote, "The weapons we fight with are not the weapons of the world. On the contrary, they have divine power to demolish strongholds" (2 Corinthians 10:4).

The book of Revelation says of the saints' battle against Satan, "They overcame him by the blood of the Lamb and by the word of their testimony . . ." (Revelation 12:11).

Second, if you are not a Christian—if you are still in arms against the Lord Jesus Christ, the rightful ruler of this world and all in it—you must remember that the victory won by the Jews at Jericho, followed by the destruction of the entire city, is a picture of what will surely come to you in the day of God's judgment. You have shut your heart against God. You have manned the battlements of your life, and although you are trembling, you refuse to repent of your sin and turn to God for his cleansing. What folly! How can you hope to stand against the only sovereign God of this universe? If you do not come to terms with God now, if you continue to hold out, you will perish in the final judgment, and your doom will be just.

The Bible says, "Kiss the Son, lest he be angry and you be destroyed in your way . . ." (Psalms 2:12).

Rahab did that. The Bible says that the Jewish armies "burned the whole city and everything in it. . . . But Joshua spared Rahab the prostitute, with her family and all who belonged to her, because she hid the men Joshua had sent as spies to Jericho . . ." (Joshua 6:24, 25). Her position was neither better nor worse than yours, and she was saved. Why should her experience not be yours? Why should you, too, not escape wrath through faith in the God of Israel?

Chapter Seven

Sin in the Camp
Joshua 7:1–8:29

Then Joshua tore his clothes and fell facedown to the ground before the ark of the LORD, remaining there till evening. The elders of Israel did the same, and sprinkled dust on their heads. And Joshua said, "Ah, Sovereign LORD, why did you ever bring this people across the Jordan to deliver us into the hands of the Amorites to destroy us? If only we had been content to stay on the other side of the Jordan! O Lord, what can I say, now that Israel has been routed by its enemies? The Canaanites and the other people of the country will hear about this and they will surround us and wipe out our name from the earth. What then will you do for your own great name?"

The LORD said to Joshua, "Stand up! What are you doing down on your face? Israel has sinned; they have violated my covenant, which I commanded them to keep. They have taken some of the devoted things; they have stolen, they have lied, they have put them with their own possessions. That is why the Israelites cannot stand against their enemies; they turn their backs and run because they have been made liable to destruction. I will not be with you anymore unless you destroy whatever among you is devoted to destruction."

Joshua 7:6–12

77

What a short step there is between a great victory and a great defeat. One moment we are riding high on the cloud of some great spiritual success. The next moment we are plunged into the dark valley of some grim spiritual failure. One moment we are Elijah standing on Mount Carmel, calling down fire on God's altar. The next moment we are Elijah at Horeb, complaining to God: ". . . I am the only one left, and now they are trying to kill me too" (1 Kings 19:10).

It is that way in Joshua. When people think of Joshua, most think of the victory of the armies of Israel at Jericho, that great walled city that stood at the entrance to the Promised Land. It is right that they do. The victory of the Israelites at Jericho was a great victory, carried out in strict obedience to the battle plan of God and accomplished by his power in throwing down the city's towering stone ramparts. But that is chapter 6. Joshua 7:1–5 tells of the army's terrible defeat at Ai, a much smaller city. It is the only defeat of the invading forces recorded in Joshua, and it contains the only report of Jews actually slain in combat. What caused such a change? How could a defeat like this follow so closely after a great victory?

Commentators have offered several explanations.

Some have suggested the Israelites were too *self-confident,* which is certainly evident in the story. Ai was a smaller city than Jericho, so the argument was advanced: "Not all the people will have to go up against Ai. Send two or three thousand men to take it and do not weary all the people, for only a few men are there" (v. 3). The people had forgotten that it was God who had delivered Jericho to them and not the Jewish troops.

Others have thought that the defeat at Ai was due to a *lack of prayer,* particularly on the part of Joshua, who should have consulted the Lord for the ordering of the battle at Ai. Apparently he did not do this. He acted on the recommendations of his scouts.

As we read the account of Israel's defeat at Ai, we sense that each of these elements was indeed present, as the commentators suggest. But these are not the reasons God himself gives for the disaster. God's explanation was that there was *sin in Israel's camp.* After the defeat and the understandable dismay of Joshua, who prostrated himself before the Lord, asking, "Ah, Sovereign LORD, why did you ever bring this people across the Jordan to deliver us into the hands of the Amorites to destroy us?" (Joshua 7:7). God replied: "Stand up! What are you doing down on your face? Israel has sinned; they have violated my covenant, which I commanded them to keep. They have taken some of the devoted things; they have stolen, they have lied, they have put them with their own possessions. That is why the Israelites cannot stand against their enemies . . ." (Joshua 7:10–12).

We must learn from this that God takes sin seriously, even if we do not, and that sin is the real cause of defeat for God's people.

Sin's Birth and Progress

What happened to Achan is recorded for our edification, to show us how sin starts and progresses if it is not confessed early and forsaken.

Achan was one of Israel's soldiers in the battle of Jericho. He was on the right side in the conflict, but he was not obedient. One of God's commands was that the entire city of Jericho be destroyed. All metal articles (gold, silver, bronze, iron) were to be taken to the treasury of the Lord as the firstfruits of the conquest, but everything else was to be consumed by fire. The people were to be killed. Achan heard those commands along with everyone else. But when he entered the city and actually saw some of the forbidden spoil before him, he coveted what he saw and took it. As he later confessed before Joshua, "When I saw in the plunder a beautiful robe from Babylonia, two hundred shekels of silver and a wedge of gold weighing fifty shekels, I coveted them and took them. They are hidden in the ground inside my tent, with the silver underneath'' (v. 21). The fact that Achan hid the plunder shows that he knew he was doing wrong. It was for this willful sin that the judgment of God came upon the whole people in the next military encounter.

What was it that led Achan to this sad act of disobedience? I suggest the following root elements.

Achan was dissatisfied. That is, he was dissatisfied with the way God had ordered the affairs of his life. It is true that God was in the process of leading Achan, along with the other members of the nation, into a new land of great wealth and opportunity. It was a country in which each family was to possess its own land, own its own house, and sit beneath its own vines and fig tree. But Achan's mind was not on the blessings that lay ahead. He was thinking of the past and was probably reasoning like this: ''God has not treated us very well in these last years of wandering. It is true that he has given us manna to eat and that he has kept our clothes from wearing out all this long time. But can you imagine how awful it is to wear the same clothes for forty years and eat the same food day after day and never have any real money to save up for the future? I have had enough of this life. Following God may satisfy these others, but it does not satisfy me. The first chance I get, I am going to improve my situation.''

Achan's dissatisfaction, which was itself a sin, gave birth to disobedience.

This is usually the case. When Satan sinned by rebelling against God, it was dissatisfaction with his position in God's world that led him to it. He was the creature; God was the Creator. But he wanted to be like God. He said, ''I will ascend to heaven; I will raise my throne above the stars of God; I will sit enthroned on the mount of assembly, on the utmost heights of the sacred mountain. I will ascend above the tops of the clouds; I will make myself like the Most High'' (Isaiah 14:13, 14). Dissatisfaction was the root of Satan's sin, and it was through his rebellion against God, who had made him what he was, that sin entered the universe.

It was the same in the case of Adam and Eve, when sin first entered the human family. God made Eve and Adam perfect in all respects. But when Satan called Eve's attention to the fact that she and her husband were not ". . . like God, knowing good and evil" (Genesis 3:5), he sowed the seed of dissatisfaction and laid the ground for his triumph.

Is this not our case also? I am not suggesting that any follower of Christ should be satisfied with a second-rate course of discipleship, still less with disobedience. There is a proper form of spiritual ambition. Even the apostle Paul said, ". . . Forgetting what is behind and straining toward what is ahead, I press on toward the goal to win the prize for which God has called me heavenward in Christ Jesus" (Philippians 3:13, 14). But this very apostle, in the same letter in which he spoke of pressing forward to win the prize of Christ's calling, also said, ". . . I have learned the secret of being content in any and every situation, whether well fed or hungry, whether living in plenty or in want" (Philippians 4:12). Paul's secret was to strive for Christ's glory rather than his own and to be willing to achieve that end through whatever means God proposed for him.

Achan coveted what was not his. Under the rules of war, a conqueror can seize the possessions of the one he defeats, and perhaps Achan was thinking along these lines. But this was his error. Achan may have been part of the invading army and may have wielded his sword effectively, but he was not the conqueror of Jericho. Nor were the other Jewish soldiers conquerors. God was the conqueror. God was giving the city of Jericho to Israel's armies, and it was he (not Joshua or any of the other generals) who had demanded that spoil from the battle go into the temple treasury and that everything else be destroyed. That is why God explained the defeat to Joshua by saying, ". . . They have taken some of the *devoted* things; they have *stolen,* they have lied, they have put them with their *own* possessions" (Joshua 7:11, emphasis mine).

In his valuable commentary on Joshua, Francis Schaeffer commented wisely on the nature of the items Achan took. He took two kinds of things: gold and silver, which suggest the sin of materialism on Achan's part, and "a beautiful robe from Babylonia," which suggests a desire to be fashionable, successful, or chic. Babylon was a highly regarded city. In later years it was overwhelmingly powerful; indeed, it overpowered Israel in 586 B.C. Even in this period of history, Babylonian material was regarded as extraordinary or fashionable. When Achan saw the robe displaying the intricate work and style of Babylon, he saw a chance to be like the world in its outwardly visible success and fashion, and therefore took the garment.[1]

We need not labor to apply this step in Achan's fall to our own lives, since materialism and worldliness are perhaps our own age's two most apparent sins. We do need to root out covetousness from our lives. "You shall not covet" is the tenth of the Ten Commandments. It is the root sin behind each of the other violations. Nothing will so quickly destroy a Christian's life as dissatisfaction with God's arrangements for him or her, which leads to lust for what God has not yet given or has given to someone else.

Achan stole the articles.   That is, Achan's dissatisfaction and covetousness, which are internal, invisible failings, led to sinful actions. Achan stole; he dissembled (he hid the precious metals and the garment); he lied. That is always the way it is. We may sin in our minds and then by the grace of God be led to confess and repudiate the sin before we reap sin's consequences. But if we do not repent of hidden sin, it will inevitably break out into the open. James says, "When tempted, no one should say, 'God is tempting

1. Francis A. Schaeffer, *Joshua and the Flow of Biblical History* (Downers Grove, Ill.: InterVarsity Press, 1975), pp. 111, 112.

me.' For God cannot be tempted by evil, nor does he tempt anyone; but each one is tempted when, by his own evil desire, he is dragged away and enticed. Then, after desire has conceived, it gives birth to sin; and sin, when it is full-grown, gives birth to death'' (James 1:13–15). This dreadful working out of sin should make us guard against even the most "innocent" dissatisfactions.

God's Judgment and New Blessing

The Bible tells us that one day the secret sins of life are going to be brought to light at the final judgment. But it does not always take that long for sin to be exposed. It took only a few minutes in the case of Achan. At God's command, lots were drawn by which one tribe out of the twelve Jewish tribes was selected, then one clan out of the numerous clans of that tribe, followed by one out of the families of that clan, and finally by one person out of the various people in that family. The chosen person was Achan of the family of Zimri, of the clan of Zerah, of the tribe of Judah.

"Tell me what you have done; do not hide it from me," Joshua said to Achan.

Achan replied, "It is true! I have sinned against the LORD, the God of Israel. This is what I have done: When I saw in the plunder a beautiful robe from Babylonia, two hundred shekels of silver and a wedge of gold weighing fifty shekels, I coveted them and took them. They are hidden in the ground inside my tent, with the silver underneath" (Joshua 7:20, 21).

The story then continues in what I think are the most chilling words of the account: "So Joshua sent messengers, and they ran to the tent, and *there it was,* hidden in his tent, with the silver underneath. They took the things from the tent, brought them to Joshua and all the Israelites and spread them out *before the LORD* (vv. 22, 23, emphasis mine).

The stolen objects were displayed before the people. But the most frightening part of the story is that they were spread out before the Lord. They were spread before the eyes of the holy God, as all sin will be.

The story ends with the death of Achan as the people of Israel stoned him (and apparently his entire family) as punishment for the sin that brought defeat on the army and dishonor to the name of God. After this, the blessing of God returned to Israel and Ai was destroyed.

Here is where Francis Schaeffer finds still another great continuity in this Old Testament book. Joshua is, as we have seen, a bridge between the years of wandering and the years of settlement, between preparation and possession. Earlier Schaeffer spoke of: the existence of the written Word of God; evidence of the unchanging power of God; and the presence of the supernatural leader. To this he added the continuity of the covenant. Here there is a continuity of judgment. When Achan sinned, the blessing of God stopped for the people corporately; when judgment was applied, blessing returned and victory followed.

Schaeffer writes,

> This simple yet profound process explains all the rest of the Old Testament. It explains the period of the judges, the period of kings, the captivities under Assyria and Babylon, the Jews' return from Babylon and the Jews' dispersion in A.D. 70 under Titus. It explains Romans 9–11, which speaks of the Jews turning away from God and yet at a future day coming back to God and once more, as a nation, being the people of God. First comes blessing, then sin enters, then comes judgment. If the people of God return to him after the judgment, the blessing begins again and flows on.
>
> This process is as much a universal as any continuity we have studied so far. It is the principle of God's judgment of his people. It is unchanging throughout Scripture because God really is there. God is a holy God, God loves his people, and God deals with his people consistently.[2]

2. Ibid., pp. 113, 114. *See also* chapters 2, 3.

This continuity extends to our own time, also. In the New Testament we see the principle in the story of Ananias and Sapphira, who were judged by God for their sin of lying to the leaders of the early church about the sale of their land and the gift of a portion of that to God's work. In our time we see it in the defeated and discouraged lives of many who have sinned but who have never brought their sin to God for cleansing.

Door of Hope

If the story of Achan and the defeat of the Jewish armies at Ai means anything to us, it must mean that sin cannot be tolerated in the Christian life. But although this is a story of judgment, it is also a proclamation of hope for the blessing that will come again when sin is repudiated.

Let me remind you of something that occurs in the book of the minor prophet Hosea. Like the seventh chapter of Joshua, Hosea is a story of God's judgment. It is the story of judgment in the life of the unfaithful wife Hosea married, a wife whose betrayal of Hosea represented the unfaithful actions of the people of Israel during the days of Hosea's ministry. In the story of the judgment of God on Gomer (Hosea's wife) the grimmest part is where God speaks of three judgments. Each one is prefaced with the word *therefore,* which makes them more or less parallel. Because of her unfaithfulness, God warns that he is going to do three things. First, he is going to ". . . block her path with thornbushes; . . ." and "wall her in so that she cannot find her way" (Hosea 2:6). This means that God was going to bring her up short so that she could not obtain her desires, just as he does with us when we choose the path of disobedience rather than discipleship.

Second, God says that he is going to ". . . take away my grain when it ripens, and my new wine when it is ready . . ." (Hosea 2:9). It means that God will begin to deprive his disobedient child of necessities.

The third time the word *therefore* occurs, it is linked to the Valley of Achor (Hosea 2:15) a direct reference to the story of Achan and his death by stoning. *Achan* and *Achor* are spelled alike, and the place of Achan's death was called Achor—a pun on his name—because *Achor* means "trouble" or "disaster," which is what Achan brought upon Israel and received back on his own head. At the time of his stoning, "Joshua said, 'Why have you brought this disaster [this *achor*] on us? The LORD will bring disaster [*achor*] on you today' " (Joshua 7:25).

When we come to this point in the story, we are frightened. The Valley of Achor was a place of death, and this seems to be the point to which the judgments on Gomer have been heading: first frustration, then deprivation. What is left but the ultimate judgment, the death of the one who has been sinning?

But right here, the inexplicable grace and mercy of God come in. For although we expect the worst, what the text actually says at this point is: "Therefore I am now going to allure her; I will lead her into the desert and speak tenderly to her. There I will give her back her vineyards, and will make *the Valley of Achor a door of hope*. There she will sing as in the days of her youth, as in the day she came up out of Egypt" (Hosea 2:14, 15, emphasis mine). Does sin bring judgment? Of course it does. This is the teaching of Scripture from the beginning of Genesis to the end of Revelation. This is why we must never take sin lightly. But judgment is not the whole story. Sin does bring judgment, but God often graciously uses the judgment to bring about change in us that enables him to turn what otherwise would be the greatest of all judgments into blessed hope.

Who can turn the Valley of Achor into a door of hope? We certainly cannot do it. But there is one who does: Jesus. He has done it by taking Achor's trouble upon himself. He was troubled for us. He went down into that dark valley of judgment, dying in our place, in order that he might raise us up in hope by his resurrection.

Chapter Eight

Mount Ebal and Mount Gerizim
Joshua 8:30–35

Then Joshua built on Mount Ebal an altar to the LORD, the God of Israel, as Moses the servant of the LORD had commanded the Israelites. He built it according to what is written in the Book of the Law of Moses—an altar of uncut stones, on which no iron tool had been used. On it they offered to the LORD burnt offerings and sacrificed fellowship offerings. There in the presence of the Israelites, Joshua copied on stones the law of Moses, which he had written. All Israel, aliens and citizens alike, with their elders, officials and judges, were standing on both sides of the ark of the covenant of the LORD, facing those who carried it—the priests, who were Levites. Half of the people stood in front of Mount Gerizim and half of them in front of Mount Ebal, as Moses the servant of the LORD had formerly commanded when he gave instructions to bless the people of Israel.

Afterward, Joshua read all the words of the law—the blessings and the curses—just as it is written in the Book of the Law. There was not a word of all that Moses had commanded that Joshua did not read to the whole assembly of Israel, including the women and children, and the aliens who lived among them.

Joshua 8:30–35

It is agreed among most students of the Old Testament that the heart of the Old Testament law is Deuteronomy and that the heart of Deuteronomy is the list of blessings and curses found in Deuteronomy 27–30. Deuteronomy presupposes the unconditional covenant of God with Abraham by which the Jews were chosen to be God's people. But it moves on from this fixed point to show that blessing or lack of blessing depends upon obedience. This is unfolded in the middle chapters. On the one hand, there is a list of curses for those who disobey God's law (Deuteronomy 27, 28). On the other hand, there is a list of blessings for those who adhere to it (Deuteronomy 28). These sections are followed by two chapters that call for a renewal of the covenant and end with a call to the people to choose the way of God's blessing.

Moses says, "This day I call heaven and earth as witnesses against you that I have set before you life and death, blessings and curses. Now choose life, so that you and your children may live and that you may love the LORD your God, listen to his voice, and hold fast to him . . ." (Deuteronomy 30:19, 20). This is the last challenge the people heard before they crossed over the Jordan River into the Promised Land.

Curses and Blessings

It is an interesting feature of this listing of curses and blessings that it was not only preached to the Jewish people by Moses before the beginning of their conquest of Canaan but that it was also repeated in a special, ceremonial way once they were in the new land. Moses had never been in Canaan, but he knew something about it, either by report or revelation. So he said that when the people of Israel came into the land, they were to read these blessings and curses at a special assembly on the sides of Mount Ebal and Mount Gerizim. Joshua did this.

Ai stood at the high western end of the approach to the hill country from the Jordan. In order to conquer Canaan, the Jewish armies had to control the mountain road running north and south through its highest regions, and in order to take the road, they had to move upward to it past Jericho and Ai. Jericho controlled the approach from the east, from the lower area of the Jordan River. Ai controlled the higher western end of this approach.

After their victories at Jericho and Ai, an observer might have expected the Jewish troops to proceed immediately with the conquest of the country by moving south along the mountain road to attack the most heavily fortified cities of that region. This is what the people did do eventually, though not at once. Instead, the observer would have seen them take a detour of about twenty-five miles north and a few miles west, to a valley situated between Mount Ebal and Mount Gerizim. This is a particularly beautiful area. The mountains, which are about three thousand feet above sea level or one thousand feet above the valley between them, are quite barren. But the valley is often green, and at one place where the mountains come close together there is a natural amphitheater. F. B. Meyer describes it as a place where the mountains are hollowed out "and the limestone stratum is broken into a succession of ledges 'so as to present the appearance of a series of regular benches.' " It is "a natural amphitheatre . . . capable of containing a vast audience of people."[1] This amphitheater was the people's destination, and it was here that they camped out for the ceremony.

One feature of the place between the mountains is its fine acoustical properties. A person on one mountain can easily hear a person on the other, and both can clearly hear what goes on below. One former visitor to Palestine, Canon Tristam, told of putting two of his traveling companions on the sides of the

---

1. F. B. Meyer, *Joshua and the Land of Promise* (Fort Washington, Pa.: Christian Literature Crusade, 1977), p. 106.

opposing mountains and having them recite the Ten Commandments antiphonally. Each could hear the other perfectly.

This is what the Jewish people did at Ebal and Gerizim after defeating Ai and assuming control of the country's high road. They did it in precise obedience to the earlier commands of Moses. Moses had said, "When you have crossed the Jordan, these tribes shall stand on Mount Gerizim to bless the people: Simeon, Levi, Judah, Issachar, Joseph and Benjamin. And these tribes shall stand on Mount Ebal to pronounce curses: Reuben, Gad, Asher, Zebulun, Dan and Naphtali" (Deuteronomy 27:12, 13). The Levites were to read the curses saying:

> Cursed is the man who carves an image or casts an idol—a thing detestable to the LORD, the work of the craftsman's hands—and sets it up in secret.
> Cursed is the man who dishonors his father or his mother.
> Cursed is the man who moves his neighbor's boundary stone.
> Cursed is the man who leads the blind astray on the road.
> Cursed is the man who withholds justice from the alien, the fatherless or the widow.
> Cursed is the man who sleeps with his father's wife, for he dishonors his father's bed.
> Cursed is the man who has sexual relations with any animal.
> Cursed is the man who sleeps with his sister, the daughter of his father or the daughter of his mother.
> Cursed is the man who sleeps with his mother-in-law.
> Cursed is the man who kills his neighbor secretly.
> Cursed is the man who accepts a bribe to kill an innocent person.
> Cursed is the man who does not uphold the words of this law by carrying them out.

After each of these twelve curses, which the Levites were to read, the people were to say, "Amen" (*see* Deuteronomy 27:15–26).

Then the blessings were to be read:

If you fully obey the LORD your God and carefully follow all his commands I give you today, the LORD your God will set you high above all the nations on earth. All these blessings will come upon you and accompany you if you obey the LORD your God:

You will be blessed in the city and blessed in the country.

The fruit of your womb will be blessed, and the crops of your land and the young of your livestock—the calves of your herds and the lambs of your flocks.

Your basket and your kneading trough will be blessed.

You will be blessed when you come in and blessed when you go out.

The LORD will grant that the enemies who rise up against you will be defeated before you. They will come at you from one direction but flee from you in seven.

Deuteronomy 28:1–7

This is what Joshua enacted on the slopes of these mountains.

. . . Half of the people stood in front of Mount Gerizim and half of them in front of Mount Ebal, as Moses the servant of the LORD had formerly commanded when he gave instructions to bless the people of Israel. Afterward, Joshua read all the words of the law—the blessings and the curses—just as it is written in the Book of the Law. There was not a word of all that Moses had commanded that Joshua did not read to the whole assembly of Israel, including the women and children, and the aliens who lived among them.

Joshua 8:33–35

It must have been an impressive and moving experience. Curses upon curses if you do not obey the law! Blessings upon blessings if you do!

A Lasting Principle

The fact that this sermon was originally preached by Moses before the people entered the land and then was acted out a second time after they had entered it and were camped on the sides of mounts Ebal and Gerizim suggests that the principle of blessing for obedience and cursing for disobedience was a lasting principle grounded in the very character of God, to be seen always in his relationships to his people.

It had already been demonstrated in the case of Achan and the defeat at Ai. When the people entered the land and commenced their attack on Jericho in strict obedience to the commands of God, the result was unprecedented blessing. It was exactly what should have been expected if: (1) God was directing the battle; (2) the people were obeying God in their conduct of it; (3) God was a benevolent God and wished to bless them with victory; and (4) God was all powerful. There is no other conceivable result, given those four factors. But when the people moved up from Jericho to attack Ai and suffered an ignominious defeat, it was apparent immediately that something had gone wrong. The "wrong" was disobedience. It was only after the sin had been exposed and judgment meted out to Achan that blessing returned. It was God's intention to bless the Jews in their conquest, but that blessing was contingent on their continuing obedience to his commands. If they disobeyed, the blessing would be withdrawn and they would experience cursings instead.

This principle explains all succeeding Jewish history, as I pointed out before. Francis Schaeffer says that it explains the period of the judges and kings, the captivities under Assyria and Babylon, the Jews' return from Babylon, and the final dispersion in A.D. 70.[2] It also explains many of our experiences today.

I met a woman I had known when she was a student and attended Tenth Presbyterian Church. She had become interested in a young man who was not a Christian and, in spite of the warnings of her friends, including a long and very pointed

2. Francis A. Schaeffer, *Joshua and the Flow of Biblical History* (Downers Grove, Ill.: InterVarsity Press, 1975), p. 113.

discussion between the two of us, she married him. I lost touch with her after that. But on the occasion I am speaking of, suddenly there she was again. At first I did not recognize her, but she introduced herself and told a little about her life in the intervening years. She had been most unhappy. As we parted, she said to me, "You know, you were absolutely right. I should never have married him." This was a case of willful disobedience followed by a clear lack of blessing on her life.

The Altar on Ebal

The ceremony that was enacted on Mount Ebal and Mount Gerizim teaches more than the principle that obedience leads to blessing and disobedience to a lack of blessing in life. It also teaches God's solution to the problem of sin in any life.

If you have read Joshua 8:30–35 carefully, you will have noticed that the part of these verses that tells of the reading of the law on the slopes of the mountains (vv. 33–35) is preceded by a section that tells of the construction of an altar on which the law was written (vv. 30–32). This, too, was in exact fulfillment of the commands of God given to the people through Moses. In Deuteronomy, Moses is recorded as having said:

> When you have crossed the Jordan into the land the LORD your God is giving you, set up some large stones and coat them with plaster. Write on them all the words of this law when you have crossed over to enter the land the LORD your God is giving you, a land flowing with milk and honey, just as the LORD, the God of your fathers, promised you. And when you have crossed the Jordan, set up these stones on Mount Ebal, as I command you today, and coat them with plaster. Build there an altar to the LORD your God, an altar of stones. Do not use any iron tool upon them. Build the altar of the LORD your God with fieldstones and offer burnt offerings on it to the LORD your God. Sacrifice fellowship offerings there, eating them and

rejoicing in the presence of the LORD your God. And you shall write very clearly all the words of this law on these stones you have set up.

Deuteronomy 27:2–8

Joshua 8:30–32 is the fulfillment of this command.

> Then Joshua built on Mount Ebal an altar to the LORD, the God of Israel, as Moses the servant of the LORD had commanded the Israelites. He built it according to what is written in the Book of the Law of Moses—an altar of uncut stones, on which no iron tool had been used. On it they offered to the LORD burnt offerings and sacrificed fellowship offerings. There in the presence of the Israelites, Joshua copied on stones the law of Moses, which he had written.

This is an absolutely fabulous thing, for at least three reasons.

First, on this great occasion when the law of Moses was so forcefully and visibly held before the people (both by the writing on stone and by the reciting of the law by the Levites and the response of the people to the Levites' reading), the altar was also constructed as the solution to the problem of those who should hear the law but who had not kept it. That is to say, it was God's solution to the sin problem. This is what God had been teaching all along. When God first gave the law on Sinai, at the same time he gave the regulations regarding sacrifices. When he gave Moses as lawgiver, at the same time he gave Aaron to be the high priest. It was as if God were thundering from Sinai, "Thou shalt not . . ." but then immediately added, "But I know you will, and so here is the way to escape condemnation."

Sin brings judgment. The judgment of sin is death. But the sacrifices show that it is possible for an innocent victim to die in place of the sinner. In those ancient days, the victim was an animal. But the animal pointed forward to the only truly sufficient sacrifice, the sacrifice of Jesus Christ. It is by faith in his death for us that we escape sin's punishment.

Second, when the altar was constructed by Joshua in obedience to the commands of Moses, it was not constructed in the valley between the two mountains, or on Mount Gerizim, but on Mount Ebal. Why was it constructed on Mount Ebal? The answer, which we find in Deuteronomy 27:12, 13, is that Ebal was the mountain from which the curses were to be read, while Gerizim was the mountain from which the blessings on the upright were declared. In other words, the altar was for sinners. It was for those who acknowledged their sin and who came, not as the righteous, but as sinners to the place of sacrifice.

It is interesting that a thousand years later, the Samaritans built their altar on Gerizim, not Ebal. So when the woman of Samaria told Jesus, "Our fathers worshiped on this mountain, but you Jews claim that the place where we must worship is in Jerusalem," she was pointing to Gerizim (John 4:20). Jesus responded by turning her away from that mountain (as well as from Mount Zion) to himself and his coming sacrifice. The chief characteristic of the Samaritans of that day *and of our day* (they still exist) is self-righteousness. The Samaritans would not come to God as sinners, confessing their need of a cleansing, substitutionary sacrifice. They came as righteous people. Consequently, the first thing Jesus did with the woman was to expose her spiritual ignorance ("You Samaritans worship what you do not know . . ." v. 22) and uncover her sin (". . . You have had five husbands, and the man you now have is not your husband . . ." [v. 18]).

Finally, the altar constructed on Mount Ebal was to be of natural stones with no human workmanship added to them. Francis Schaeffer, who is excellent on this point, rightly calls this principle "a complete negation of all humanism."[3] That is, it is a denial of the thought that human beings can add anything at all

3. Ibid., p. 123.

to salvation. They cannot. Salvation is by grace through the work of God alone.

It is not just a matter of coming to God as a sinner, thereby taking your place, as it were, on Mount Ebal. That is absolutely essential—there is no place for the self-righteous in God's presence—but it is not enough. Nor is it enough even to come to the place of sacrifice, thereby acknowledging your need of another to die for you. In addition to these absolutely essential things, it is also necessary to come acknowledging that there is nothing, absolutely nothing, that you can contribute to the effort.

The Reformers expressed this truth by the phrases *sola fide* and *sola gratia*. *Sola fide* means ''by faith alone''; that is, faith in the work of God alone and not faith that is in any way linked to human merit. *Sola gratia* means ''by grace alone''; that is, grace entirely. Augustus Toplady put it like this:

> Nothing in my hand I bring,
> Simply to thy cross I cling;
> Naked, come to thee for dress,
> Helpless, look to thee for grace;
> Foul, I to the Fountain fly;
> Wash me, Savior, or I die.
>
> Rock of Ages, cleft for me,
> Let me hide myself in thee.

Christ's cross is that Fountain. He is the rock, cleft for us. If we come to him, we will have shelter and cleansing—and also receive power to begin to live in a way that brings blessing.

Chapter Nine

The Error of Walking by Sight
Joshua 9:1–27

When the people of Gibeon heard what Joshua had done to Jericho and Ai, they resorted to a ruse: They went as a delegation whose donkeys were loaded with worn-out sacks and old wineskins, cracked and mended. The men put worn and patched sandals on their feet and wore old clothes. All the bread of their food supply was dry and moldy. Then they went to Joshua in the camp at Gilgal and said to him and the men of Israel, "We have come from a distant country; make a treaty with us. . . ."

The men of Israel sampled their provisions but did not inquire of the LORD. Then Joshua made a treaty of peace with them to let them live, and the leaders of the assembly ratified it by oath.

Three days after they had made the treaty with the Gibeonites, the Israelites heard that they were neighbors, living near them.

Joshua 9:3–6, 14–16

It is hard not to admire the Gibeonites. What would you have done had you been in their place? They were residents of a mountain stronghold in Canaan, perhaps the next city in the terrifying line of Jewish march. They had heard of the destruction of Jericho and Ai and the ruthless extermination of all who had lived there. So, being afraid, they resorted to deception, judging that they would not be able to stand against the Israelite forces militarily. They donned old clothes, loaded their animals with worn-out sacks filled with dry and moldy bread, hung cracked wineskins on their donkeys, and came to Joshua and the other leaders of Israel, asking that a treaty be made with them. Their disguise was an attempt to convince the Jews that they had come from far away and that there would be nothing wrong with their being treated as allies rather than as enemies who could not be permitted to live. As I say, it is hard not to admire them.

It is also hard not to sympathize with, even if not quite admire, the Israelites. The Gibeonites' disguise was good, after all, and the Jews were probably moved by humanitarian concerns. True, they were suspicious. They said, "Perhaps you live near us. How then can we make a treaty with you?" (Joshua 9:7). But there was the moldy bread. There were the broken wineskins. The clothes were old. The sandals were worn out with much walking. Besides, the alternative to believing and sparing these visitors was to disbelieve and kill them. What harm could there be in making a treaty?

To admire the Gibeonites and sympathize with the Israelites is natural. But it only shows how far we are from doing things God's way naturally. The Bible's judgment of the Jews' action was that they ". . . did not inquire of the LORD" and so erred greatly (v. 14).

The Error of Sight

The Jews trusted to their own natural understanding, based on observation, and our natural reaction is to say, "But what's wrong with that? Is it really possible to operate any other way? Our world is a world of sense impressions. They are all we have to go on. We have to decide on the basis of what we see and hear and touch, and if in operating that way we make mistakes, we can hardly be blamed for them. There is nothing else to be done.''

The great error here—I am sure you can see it—is assuming that reality is nothing more than the material. It is true that much of reality *is* material. That is why judgments based on sense impressions are proper and reliable under many circumstances. When you pull a piece of meat out of the refrigerator and find that it is discolored and has a bad smell, it is wrong to eat it. Your senses are given to you by God to tell you that the meat is bad and that you will probably get sick if you eat it. That way of making a decision works for us every day in scores of situations. But the difficulty with operating that way all the time is that reality does not consist only of the material. There is a spiritual world, too, and in that spiritual world there is a powerful, crafty, and malicious being who is bent on our destruction. We cannot see the devil. We cannot handle, taste, or smell his stratagems. Therefore, in all spiritual (and all moral) areas, we need wisdom that goes beyond any we can derive from sense impressions.

This is what that often-quoted advice from Proverbs is all about. ''Trust in the LORD with all your heart and lean not on your own understanding; in all your ways acknowledge him, and he will make your paths straight'' (Proverbs 3:5, 6). The key words are *lean not on your own understanding.*

I think Alan Redpath overstates the case slightly when he uses the word *anything.* In many instances, mere sense impressions are right. But he is still largely on target when he says:

> Never, *never,* NEVER trust your own judgment in anything. When common sense says that a course is right, lift your heart to God, for the path of faith and the path of blessing may be in a direction completely opposite to that which you call common sense. When voices tell you that action is urgent, that something must be done immediately, refer everything to the tribunal of heaven. Then, if you are still in doubt, dare to stand

still. If you are called on to act and you have not time to pray, don't act. If you are called on to move in a certain direction and cannot wait until you have peace with God about it, don't move. Be strong enough and brave enough to dare to stand and wait on God, for none of them that wait on him shall ever be ashamed. That is the only way to outmatch the devil.[1]

We need to be very specific about this. If we are to live for God in this world, we must recognize that there is a spiritual realm as well as a material one, and we must seek God's strength to be successful in the battles that take place there.

Let me remind you of the sixth chapter of Ephesians where Paul writes of our struggles in terms of a military metaphor:

> Finally, be strong in the Lord and in his mighty power. Put on the full armor of God so that you can take your stand against the devil's schemes. For our struggle is not against flesh and blood, but against the rulers, against the authorities, against the powers of this dark world and against the spiritual forces of evil in the heavenly realms. Therefore put on the full armor of God, so that when the day of evil comes, you may be able to stand your ground, and after you have done everything, to stand. Stand firm then, with the belt of truth buckled around your waist, with the breastplate of righteousness in place, and with your feet fitted with the readiness that comes from the gospel of peace. In addition to all this, take up the shield of faith, with which you can extinguish all the flaming arrows of the evil one. Take the helmet of salvation and the sword of the Spirit, which is the word of God. And pray in the Spirit on all occasions with all kinds of prayers and requests. . . .
>
> Ephesians 6:10–18

These verses may be summarized by a number of important principles.

1. Alan Redpath, *Victorious Christian Living: Studies in the Book of Joshua* (Westwood, N. J.: Fleming H. Revell Co., 1955), pp. 142, 143.

1. As Christians *we are involved in spiritual warfare*. This was true for the Jewish armies in their conquest, even though their warfare was also physical and they may not always have been fully aware of its spiritual dimensions. It is obviously much truer of us who are commissioned to bear the gospel of the light of God in Jesus Christ to pagan darkness.

2. To be successful in this warfare *we must be clothed with spiritual armor*. This indicates that it is not only a case of our being sent to attack the enemy; the enemy is also attacking us, and we must be protected against his schemes. As Paul states it, we need truth, righteousness, knowledge of the gospel, and faith. The latter especially is to fend off Satan's arrows.

3. *Our offensive weapon is the word of God*. This is what Joshua and the other leaders of Israel lacked in the case of the men of Gibeon: a word from God. Up to this point, everything the nation did was connected in some way with a specific divine revelation. God told the people when to cross the Jordan, what to do after they had crossed it, how to attack Jericho, and so on. Even in the case of Ai, although there had been sin in the camp originally, there were still divine instructions as to how the ambush should be laid and what should be done with the city following its capture. In this chapter there is no word from the Lord at all, *because the people did not seek it*.

Do you lack a word from God in the decisions you face? If so, it is because you are not seeking it. The Bible says, "If any of you lacks wisdom, he should ask God, who gives generously to all without finding fault, and it will be given to him" (James 1:5).

4. *We are to pray* constantly for the help and blessing of God. Paul says, ". . . on all occasions with all kinds of prayers and requests . . ." (Ephesians 6:18). The people of Israel failed to do this and so erred greatly.

The Consequences of Error

How quickly they found out! I do not know how long the Gibeonites spent in their preparation of this ruse or how long the

Israelites spent in examining their belongings, discussing the problem, and eventually deciding to make a treaty with them. No doubt each group took what it considered to be sufficient time, perhaps weeks in the first instance, days in the second. Yet the text is striking when it says in Joshua 9:16 (immediately after the verse that says, "Then Joshua made a treaty of peace with them to let them live, and the leaders of the assembly ratified it by oath"), "Three days after they made the treaty with the Gibeonites, the Israelites heard that they were neighbors, living near them."

Three days to discover their error!

But a lifetime to live with it!

The story tells us that when the people learned that the Gibeonites were actually from quite close at hand, they grumbled against their leaders, judging them to be responsible. Presumably they wanted to kill the Gibeonites regardless of the treaty. But although the leaders had erred in the first place in failing to consult the Lord about the Gibeonites, trusting rather in their own sense impressions and judgment, they did not err again by repudiating their covenant as the people wanted. They recognized the importance of their oath and replied, "We have given them our oath by the LORD, the God of Israel, and we cannot touch them now. This is what we will do to them: We will let them live, so that wrath will not fall on us for breaking the oath we swore to them" (vv. 19, 20). So they let the Gibeonites live, and the leaders' promise to them was respected.

It was respected for centuries. On a later occasion, when Saul, a king of Israel, broke the covenant by killing large numbers of the Gibeonites, God sided with the Gibeonites and brought judgment upon Israel. Second Samuel 21:1 records that there was a three-year famine in Israel because Saul "put the Gibeonites to death." It was removed only after the house of Saul was judged by an arrangement between the surviving Gibeonites and King David (*see* 2 Samuel 21:1–14).

This is the great problem with a failure to consult the Lord in all matters: We must live with the consequences of our wrong actions. "Can't a sin or wrong action be forgiven?" someone asks. Yes, of course. But the consequences of that false step must often be lived with indefinitely.

The obvious example here is marriage, although many other examples could be given. Often a Christian will marry one who is not God's choice for him or her. Frequently the mistake involves a non-Christian, but the same thing can happen with two followers of the Lord. What can be done in such circumstances? The world has an answer. It says, "Get a divorce. You have to do what is best for youself. Think of your future." God's Word says that this is something with which the Christian (or Christians) must live. Paul wrote, ". . . A wife must not separate from her husband. . . . And a husband must not divorce his wife" (1 Corinthians 7:10, 11). Above all, there must be no remarriage. Jesus said, "Anyone who divorces his wife and marries another woman commits adultery against her. And if she divorces her husband and marries another man, she commits adultery" (Mark 10:11, 12).

But what about the world's solution of getting out of a bad marriage? "Certainly you can escape the consequences of your original bad decision in that way," someone says. Can you? The true answer is that you cannot. You change one set of consequences for another, but you do not escape bad consequences. In this situation, the results affect whatever children there may be, the couple's friends, and even the new marriage.

God of Circumstances

Disobedience is no solution to the bad consequences of an earlier disobedience. But obedience often *is* a solution. At least it provides conditions in which God frequently does the unexpected.

This was the case with the Gibeonites. They had deceived Israel by pretending to have come from a distant land when they were actually from nearby, and they suffered the consequences of that deception. Their lives were spared, which was their objective, but they were made servants or slaves. The text says ". . . woodcutters and water carriers for the entire community . . ." (Joshua 9:21). Yes, but let your eye run down to Joshua 9:27, where we find the phrase with this significant addition: "and for the altar of the LORD at the place the LORD would choose." I think that is tremendous! The Gibeonites were made servants to the Jews, but the place of their service was specifically said to be (at least in part) at the altar of the Lord. In other words, although servants, they had the privilege of being brought close to spiritual things on a regular basis. In later years, when the Jews went off after false gods, the Gibeonites would still be standing at the altar where the true God had ordained that sacrifices should be made for sins.

It was an appropriate blessing for people who had explained their coming to Joshua by saying, "Your servants have come from a very distant country because of the fame of the LORD your God. For we have heard reports of him: all that he did in Egypt, and all that he did to the two kings of the Amorites east of the Jordan—Sihon king of Heshbon, and Og king of Bashan, who reigned in Ashtaroth" (Joshua 9:9, 10).

Francis Schaeffer compares the Gibeonites to the prostitute Rahab at this point, noting that although the Gibeonites' testimony was not as clear as Rahab's—she said, ". . . The LORD your God is God in heaven above and on the earth below" (Joshua 2:11)—they nevertheless believed what they had heard and came because of the power of the Jewish God. Schaeffer writes:

> In Semitic usage a name is a verbalization which represents one's entire character. What the Gibeonites were really saying

was "We came because of who the Lord your God is."
Similarly, they spoke of "How that the Lord thy God
commanded his servant Moses" (Joshua 9:24). So in the cases
of both Rahab and the Gibeonites what they had heard was
sufficient to convince them. Rahab left the kingdom of the
enemies of God for the kingdom of the Jews. In making her
decision, she pitted herself against her king and her culture.
The Gibeonites did likewise. They broke with the confederacy
and came over to the people of God. Further, Rahab's act
means that if her old king had found out what she had done he
would undoubtedly have killed her. The Gibeonites were
actually caught in their defection. The confederacy knew well
what they had done. The confederacy, therefore, did in fact
come against the Gibeonites to exterminate them.[2]

Schaeffer makes a point of the Gibeonites' loyalty once they
had made their decision. For many years after this incident, there
was war between the citizens of the land and the invading
Israelites. Yet never once in the record of that long conquest do
we hear of any Gibeonite defecting to his original side.

So they prospered.

When the land was divided, Gibeon was one of the cities
given to the line of Aaron. It became a special place where God
was known. Approximately four hundred years later, David
put the tabernacle in that city. This meant that the altar and the
priests were in Gibeon as well. At least one of David's mighty
men, those who were closest to him in battle, was a Gibeonite.
At that important and solemn moment when Solomon, David's
son, ascended the throne, Solomon made burnt offerings at
Gibeon. It was there he had his vision, when God spoke to him
about his coming rule. Much later still, about five hundred
years before Christ, in the time of Zerubbabel, the genealogies
of those Jews who returned from captivity under the Babylo-
nians included a list of the Gibeonites. This is especially

2. Francis A. Schaeffer, *Joshua and the Flow of Biblical History* (Downers
Grove, Ill.: InterVarsity, 1975), pp. 149, 150.

striking because the names of some who claimed to be Jews were not found in the registry, and they were not allowed to be a part of the Jewish nation. In the days of Nehemiah, the Gibeonites were mentioned as being among the people who rebuilt the walls of Jerusalem. The Gibeonites had come in among the people of God, and hundreds of years later they were still there.[3]

We, the Gibeonites

When we studied the story of Rahab, I pointed out that there are parallels between her experience and ours if we are Gentiles who have come to believe in the God of Israel through faith in the Jew, Jesus Christ. There are parallels with the Gibeonites, too. They were liars, deceivers. They were under judgment and exposed to the severe wrath of God. So also have we been. We heard of the true God, as they did. True, at the beginning we did not know very much about him. Yet God used that small beginning to draw us into the company of his people, where we learned more and were eventually fully identified with those who have been saved by faith in Jesus Christ. We, too, believed. This is a great marvel, a tribute to God's grace.

If you have not yet been drawn into the company of God's people, let what you know of the true God draw you. You need only know that he *is* the true God and that he has provided the way for you to be saved through Jesus' death. Come to him and escape the judgment.

3. Ibid., pp. 150, 151.

Chapter Ten

The Longest Day
Joshua 10:1–15

> *On the day the LORD gave the Amorites over to Israel,*
> *Joshua said to the LORD in the presence of Israel:*
> *"O sun, stand still over Gibeon,*
> *O moon, over the Valley of Aijalon."*
> *So the sun stood still,*
> *and the moon stopped,*
> *till the nation avenged itself on*
> *its enemies,*
> *as it is written in the Book of Jashar.*
> *The sun stopped in the middle of the sky and delayed*
> *going down about a full day. There has never been a day*
> *like it before or since, a day when the LORD listened to a*
> *man. Surely the LORD was fighting for Israel!*
> *Then Joshua returned with all Israel to the camp at*
> *Gilgal.*
>
> Joshua 10:12–15

There is a text in the tenth chapter of Joshua that has been used
to great effect by Leland Wong, and evangelist to Chinese people
in America. At the top of his letterhead there are phrases from
three verses: Joshua 10:13 ("The sun stood still"); 2 Kings 6:6
("The iron did float"); and Psalms 48:14 ("This God is our
God"). I have often used these verses as a testimony to the
greatness of the God of the Bible, the God who does miracles.

107

But did the iron *really* float?

Did the sun *really* stand still?

Miracles of this magnitude—particularly that the sun stood still—are so problematic to so many people that I have treated them as a separate category in a chapter titled "Alleged Problems in the Bible" in my book *Standing on the Rock*. There I say:

> If you are driving along in a car at sixty miles an hour and you suddenly slam on the brakes, you fall forward. We assume that if the earth suddenly stopped, everybody would fall over. We all recognize those difficulties. But God is certainly up to the miracle. And whether this is to be explained by appeal to pure miracle or not, there are certainly incidents in the Bible that are pure miracle and these just cannot be escaped by rationalistic explanations.[1]

Still, the stopping of the sun and moon in the days of Joshua at Gibeon is a tremendous occurrence and deserves careful handling.

"The Sun Stood Still"

The Gibeonites had made their treaty with Israel, thus saving their lives. But when the peoples of the other hilltop fortresses heard of it, they looked on the Gibeonites as traitors and quite naturally decided to move against them. The text says:

> Now Adoni-Zedek king of Jerusalem heard that Joshua had taken Ai and totally destroyed it, doing to Ai and its king as he had done to Jericho and its king, and that the people of Gibeon had made a treaty of peace with Israel and were living near them. He and his people were very much alarmed at this, . because Gibeon was an important city, like one of the royal cities; it was larger than Ai, and all its men were good fighters. So Adoni-Zedek king of Jerusalem appealed to Hoham king of Hebron, Piram king of Jarmuth, Japhia king of Lachish and

1. James Montgomery Boice, *Standing on the Rock* (Wheaton, Ill.: Tyndale House Publishers, 1978), p. 95.

Debir king of Eglon. "Come up and help me attack Gibeon,"
he said, "because it has made peace with Joshua and the
Israelites."

Joshua 10:1–5

It is a point of minor interest that this is the first mention of the
city of Jerusalem in the Bible. But to Joshua the action these
verses report meant that, for the first time in his campaign, he
would have to meet the combined forces of the Canaanites in an
open and head-on military encounter.

Or would he? According to the account, Joshua did not learn
of the Canaanite confederacy directly or from spies, but from the
Gibeonites when they were attacked. When the kings of the
Amorites moved against them, the Gibeonites sent word to
Joshua: ". . . 'Do not abandon your servants. Come up to us
quickly and save us! Help us, because all the Amorite kings from
the hill country have joined forces against us' " (Joshua 10:6). If
Joshua had been a lesser man, he might have regarded this as a
way to escape the consequences of his rash agreement to spare
the Gibeonites. He had been tricked by them. Now they were
being attacked for their perfidy. Was it not wise and would it not
be just to allow them to meet their fate unaided? If the kings of
the cities of the hill country destroyed the Gibeonites—well, this
would remove at least one problem from his hands.

Joshua did not think that way. He had made a treaty with the
Gibeonites in God's name, and now he decided it was important
to stand by the agreement. So rather than looking on the situation
as an easy way to be relieved of a difficulty, he seized it as an
opportunity. At the time the message came to him, he was at
Gilgal, his camp in the region of Jericho by the Jordan River. But
he immediately marshaled his forces, marched at night up the
steep ravine to Ai and then south to Gibeon, where he fell on the
unsuspecting Canaanite confederacy suddenly, presumably at
dawn. The move was so bold and the attack so sudden that the

armies of the hill country fled. The text says, ". . . Israel pursued them along the road going up to Beth Horon and cut them down all the way to Azekah and Makkedah" (v. 10).

Going south from Gibeon, where the battle began, there is a ten-mile ascent to Beth Horon the Upper. But from that point the road drops away precipitously, falling seven hundred feet in two miles. The rock is cut into steps, and it was down this rugged descent that the Canaanites fled before the pursuing Israelites. They were hoping to reach the fortified cities from which they had set out, seal the gates, and gain at least a night's respite before they had to face their pursuing foes again.

What a day that was! As the Canaanites fled down the precipitous rocky path, God intervened in the first of two miracles to aid the Israelites. He sent a hailstorm that struck the panicked soldiers on the slopes below Beth Horon. Hailstorms can be of fantastic proportions in the east, and this one was exceptional, even by these standards. The hailstones killed so many that, as the text says, ". . . More of them died from the hailstones than were killed by the swords of the Israelites" (v. 11).

Picture the scene that must have greeted Joshua as he crested the ridge at Beth Horon. Before him, as far as his eyes could see, were masses of the panicked armies being pusued by his own soldiers. Over the slopes and above the plains beyond, there was a great cloud from which hail was falling. To his right, the sun was beginning its long afternoon descent toward the Mediterranean. Joshua must have realized two things. First, this was an unprecedented opportunity to destroy the southern confederacy. The best of their soldiers had come out against him, and they were fleeing. If he could destroy them now, the southlands would be open to his advancing armies. At the same time, he must have recognized that the day was escaping. When the sun set, fighting would cease, and there was not enough time before sunset to achieve total victory.

So Joshua did an unprecedented thing: He asked God to prolong the day. The story says:

> On the day the LORD gave the Amorites over to Israel,
> Joshua said to the LORD in the presence of Israel:
> "O sun, stand still over Gibeon,
>   O moon, over the Valley of Aijalon."
> So the sun stood still,
>   And the moon stopped,
>   till the nation avenged itself on
>   its enemies.
>
> Joshua 10:12, 13

The text is hardly exaggerating when it continues, "There has never been a day like it before or since, a day when the LORD listened to a man. Surely the LORD was fighting for Israel!" Joshua 10:14).

What Really Happened?

But what really happened at Gibeon? Did the sun really stand still in relation to the earth, meaning that the earth slowed and then stopped its rotation? That is certainly what the text seems to say. But the physical problems associated with such a miracle are so large that conservative scholars as well as more liberal ones have searched rather widely for an alternative.

In his discussion of this problem in *The Christian View of Science and Scripture,* Bernard Ramm highlights four possible interpretations.

The words are poetical. The people of those days often wove references to the heavenly bodies into accounts of their victories, as in Judges 5:20, where Deborah and Barak claim that the very stars fought against their enemy, Sisera. According to this explanation, this is what Joshua was doing and what the text reports. Joshua saw his opportunity escaping and called on God for strength. God answered by refreshing his soldiers so much that they were able to do a day's fighting in less than half that time. So it was as if (or it actually seemed to them as if) the day had been lengthened. The Bible does use poetical language, of course. But it seems to most interpreters that this is not really the case here. Besides, there is the miracle of the hailstones. If they are poetical, what are they supposed to represent? If they are not, then why should the stopping of the sun not be taken literally, too?

The sun and moon (or earth) actually did stop.   People who believe in an omnipotent God do not have difficulty accepting the possibility of even this great miracle. Omnipotent means *"all-powerful,"* and if God is all-powerful, then he can as easily stop the sun and moon or earth as do anything. Perhaps this *is* what happened. Still, the scope of the miracle seems so great that even such a conservative commentator as Francis Schaeffer argues that God merely lengthened the hours of sunlight by some means.[2] He compares it to the lengthening of the days of summer or summer days in extremely northern countries like Norway, when the sun does not set.

A miracle of refraction of the sun's rays made it seem as if the sun and moon were out of their regular places.   This may be the kind of miracle Francis Schaeffer is thinking of. Ramm cites two articles by R. Short and J. Lowell Butler which argue this point scientifically.[3] They believe that the miracles of Joshua

2. Francis A. Schaeffer, *Joshua and the Flow of Biblical History* (Downers Grove, Ill.: InterVarsity Press, 1977), p. 142.

3. A. Rendle Short, *Modern Discovery and the Bible* (London: Intervarsity Fellowship of Evangelical Unions, 1943), p. 117, and J. Lowell Butler, "Mirages Are Light Benders," *Journal of the American Scientific Affiliation,*

10 were due to "a special and rare mirage in the earth's atmosphere which is similar to one or more of the natural mirages, but [was] of a magnitude, altitude and character that would be the result of a divine miracle only."[4]

There are two unverified claims that might have bearing here. First, some writings about this miracle report that there are Egyptian, Chinese, and Hindu records of a long day. Second, there are unconfirmed reports that "it is common knowledge among astronomers that one full day is missing in our astronomical calculations and that Professor Pickering of the Harvard observatory has traced it back to the time of Joshua."[5] From time to time I have seen claims like this myself, but I have never found any trustworthy documentation of them. Ramm likewise reports that he has been unable to verify them to his satisfaction.

Joshua did not ask for a longer day but rather for a release from the day's great heat. The Hebrew verb *dom*, which most of the English versions translate as "stand still," usually means "be silent, cease, or leave off." Because of this, E. W. Maunder of Greenwich and Robert Dick Wilson of Princeton suggested that Joshua, in the heat of the day, requested that the sun cease shining and that God's answer was the hailstorm that not only brought refreshment to his soldiers so they could do the work of a full day in half a day, but also brought destruction to his enemy.

I confess that I have no great convictions as to what happened, and as I read the various articles and books available, I sense that no one else has very strong convictions on this point, either. I do not believe the words are poetry, in spite of their having been

vol. 3 (December 1951), pp. 1–18. *See* Bernard Ramm, *The Christian View of Science and Scripture* (Grand Rapids: Wm. B. Eerdmans, 1954), p. 158.

4. Butler, "Mirages," p. 9.

5. Ramm, *Christian View of Science*, p. 159.

recorded in the book of Jashar, a largely poetical book. I doubt if the earth actually stopped its rotation, even more that the sun and moon actually stopped in their passage through space. I tend to think that other phenomena were used by God to prolong daylight, but I do not know, and all I can say is that I am content to wait until God himself reveals precisely what happened. What is certain is that God did something to give the Jewish armies a complete and decisive victory.

This God, Our God

But this is not the end of the story for us. Scripture is given for our ". . . teaching, rebuking, correcting and training in righteousness" (2 Timothy 3:16). We must ask what we are to specifically learn from the account.

The first lesson is that nothing is too great for God. A moment ago I mentioned Robert Dick Wilson, a former professor of Hebrew at Princeton Seminary. About twelve years after he had graduated from Princeton, Donald Grey Barnhouse was invited back to preach in the chapel, and when he arrived, he noticed that Wilson had taken a place near the front to hear him. When the service was over, his old Hebrew professor came up to Barnhouse and said, "If you come back again, I will not come to hear you preach. I only come once. I am glad that you are a big-godder. When my boys come back, I come to see if they are big-godders or little-godders, and then I know what their ministry will be."

Barnhouse asked Wilson to explain. He said, "Well, some men have a little god, and they are always in trouble with him. He can't do any miracles. He can't take care of the inspiration of the Scriptures and their preservation and transmission to us. They have a little god, and I call them little-godders. Then there are those who have a great God. He speaks, and it is done. He commands, and it stands fast. He knows how to show himself strong on behalf of those that fear him. You have a great God, and he will bless your ministry."[6]

Donald Barnhouse did have a great God, and he did bless his ministry. But that God is our God, too, just as he was the God of Joshua and the victorious Israelites. Nothing is too great for him.

The second lesson of Joshua 10 is that we should expect days of great personal victory in our walk with God. This was the secret of Joshua's action, of course. God had told Joshua that he was giving the kings of the hill country and their armies into his hand. ("Do not be afraid of them; I have given them into your hand. Not one of them will be able to withstand you" [v.8].) So when he saw them escaping toward their city fortresses to the south, Joshua was emboldened to call upon God and expect God's supernatural intervention. I know that we are inclined to presume on God, claiming promises that God has not given or victories that are personal and selfish and not for his glory. We have no mandate to expect God's intervention in such cases. But what about when we really are fighting for God and when we really are seeking God's glory? In cases like this, we should expect God's intervention and can call out for it.

I notice that Joshua prayed ". . . to the LORD *in the presence of Israel . . ."* (v. 12, emphasis mine). That is, he was open about his expectations. He was not afraid of being humiliated by failure, because he wanted only what God had told him would happen. He laid his belief on the line. If we do as Joshua did, we will find that God honors it.

Finally, although Joshua prayed for God's miraculous intervention in the battle, he was nevertheless not the least bit slack in his own responsibilities. Indeed, he is a faithful and superb commander throughout the story. He is faithful to his treaty with the Gibeonites. He is creative and daring in his night march from

6. Donald Grey Barnhouse, *Let Me Illustrate: Stories, Anecdotes, Illustrations* (Westwood, N. J.: Fleming H. Revell Co., 1967), pp. 132, 133.

Gilgal to attack the armies of the enemy the next morning. Then, once the battle was begun, he was rigorous in pursuing it. He did not pull back either from fatigue or from lack of will, but continued to the very end. He was victorious, and God provided him with the opportunity to achieve a total victory. Our victories may be of a very different nature, but they should nevertheless also be great victories.

Chapter Eleven

The Southern and Northern Campaigns
Joshua 10:16–12:24

So Joshua subdued the whole region, including the hill country, the Negev, the western foothills and the mountain slopes, together with all their kings. He left no survivors. He totally destroyed all who breathed, just as the LORD, the God of Israel, had commanded. Joshua subdued them from Kadesh Barnea to Gaza and from the whole region of Goshen to Gibeon. All these kings and their lands Joshua conquered in one campaign, because the LORD, the God of Israel, fought for Israel.

At that time Joshua went and destroyed the Anakites from the hill country: from Hebron, Debir and Anab, from all the hill country of Judah, and from all the hill country of Israel. Joshua totally destroyed them and their towns. No Anakites were left in Israelite territory; only in Gaza, Gath and Ashdod did any survive. So Joshua took the entire land, just as the LORD had directed Moses, and he gave it as an inheritance to Israel according to their tribal divisions.

Then the land had rest from war.

Joshua 10:40–42; 11:21–23

To the middle of the tenth chapter of Joshua, the story of the conquest of Canaan is told in detail. There have only been three real engagements: at Jericho, Ai, and on the hills near Gibeon, the last of which flowed over into a great running battle as the panicked Amorites fled south toward their fortified mountain cities. These stories have been carefully told. Now this method of recounting the invasion changes. Instead of a careful telling of the military and other details of each battle, there are quick summaries of the campaigns that led the advancing Jewish armies first south and then north throughout the land.

In all, there were three phases to the conquest. There was the initial crossing of the Jordan River, followed by a push from Jericho to Ai into the very heart of the country. This first phase established the Israelite armies in the land and divided Canaan. The second phase of the campaign was in the area south of the wedge that had been driven in from Jericho. There were many strong hill cities in this area, and it was the kings and armies of these cities that had combined to attack Gibeon and were routed by Joshua when he came to the Gibeonites' rescue. Joshua 10:29–43 tells of Joshua's mopping-up efforts in this area. The third and final phase of the invasion was the subjugation of the northern region. This campaign is recounted in Joshua 11. It is followed by a summary of the invasion, including a list of the defeated kings, in chapter twelve.

So these three chapters (Joshua 10–12) contain the heart of the conquest of Canaan by the Jewish armies.

The Southern Campaign

Apparently, the campaign against the southern cities did not take much time, as Joshua quickly moved to take advantage of his success at Gibeon.

The account begins with the calling together of the kings of the most prominent southern cities by Adoni-Zedek, king of Jerusalem, as stated at the beginning of chapter 10. Four kings joined themselves to him: Hoham, king of Hebron; Piram, king of Jarmuth; Japhia, king of Lachish; and Debir, king of Eglon.

Jerusalem was the most prominent of these hilltop city fortresses. It was only about six miles south of Gibeon and so felt the defection of the Gibeonites strongly.

Hebron lay nineteen miles south-southwest of Jerusalem. It was the place where the patriarchs had lived centuries earlier, where Abraham, Isaac, and Jacob (and their wives) lay buried, and where Joseph would eventually be buried in compliance with his final request (*see* Genesis 50:25).

Jarmuth was sixteen miles west of Jerusalem on a ridge overlooking the coastal plain and sea. Today it is called Khirbet Yarmuk.

Lachish was one of the oldest cities in Palestine, dating back to the eighth millennium B.C. It is now called Tell el-Duweir.

Eglon is usually identified with Tell el-Hesi, also a very ancient city.

The armies of these cities formed a coalition against Gibeon and were routed by Joshua as a result of his sudden and unexpected attack. They were destroyed by the pursuing Israelites as they fled southward.

What of the leaders? Joshua 10:16–28 tells how the kings of Jerusalem, Hebron, Jarmuth, Lachish, and Eglon hid in a cave near the southern city of Makkedah (the location is unknown) during their armies' rout and were discovered by Jewish soldiers. Joshua knew the importance of having discovered and captured the enemy kings, but he also knew the day's military opportunities. So he ordered the cave sealed until later while he and his soldiers continued to pursue the fleeing armies. Only after the battle was over did Joshua return to the cave, gather his army at Makkedah, and bring out the five rulers.

The next day Joshua did two things. First, he made the defeated kings lie down in the dust before him while he called the commanders of the divisions of his army to come and place their feet on the defeated kings' necks. Joshua said, "Do not be afraid; do not be discouraged. Be strong and courageous. This is what

the LORD will do to all the enemies you are going to fight''
(Joshua 10:25).

Second, Joshua killed the kings of Jerusalem, Hebron, Jarmuth, Lachish, and Eglon, and hung their bodies on trees until
nightfall.

Did I say *two* things? It is true that Joshua did two things as far
as the kings were concerned, but I find it amusing to read in
Joshua 10:28 that the same day in which he produced the kings,
killed them, and hung them on trees, Joshua also took Makkedah.
It seems he could not quite hold still. He grew bored looking at
five dead kings hanging on trees, so he redeemed the time by
taking the nearby city. The remainder of the chapter tells how he
then went on to subdue one southern stronghold after another:
Libnah, Lachish, Eglon, Hebron, and Debir. Three of those cities
had belonged to the kings he had just killed; the others were
nearby. It is significant that Jerusalem is not included in the
listing of the cities Joshua is said to have taken, although the king
of Jerusalem, Adoni-Zedek, was among those killed. Jerusalem
escaped being conquered by the Israelites (Joshua 15:63) and was
not taken until the time of David, hundreds of years later (2
Samuel 5:6, 7).

The chapter concludes by saying that Joshua totally subdued
four regions: the hill country, the Negev (the desert area to the
more distant south), the western foothills, and the mountain
slopes. ''Joshua subdued them from Kadesh Barnea to Gaza and
from the whole region of Goshen to Gibeon. All these kings and
their lands Joshua conquered in one campaign, because the LORD,
the God of Israel, fought for Israel'' (Joshua 10:41, 42).

The Northern Campaign

The final phase of the conquest of Canaan was in the north, and
again it followed the actions of the kings of the land. Jabin, king
of Hazor, was the leader of a northern coalition, just as

Adoni-Zedek, king of Jerusalem, had been the leader in the south. He was alarmed at the Jewish victories, as well he should have been, so he called the kings and armies of the northern cities together. These joined forces near the Waters of Merom, a lake a little north of the larger Sea of Galilee.

The new element in this battle was the use of chariots by the coalition. I do not know how accurate Josephus, the Jewish historian, is at this point, since he wrote so many hundreds of years later, but according to him, the combined forces of the Canaanites numbered 300,000 foot soldiers, 100,000 cavalry, and 20,000 chariots. If this was so (or even if it is only an approximation of the size of the army), this must have been the greatest engagement of Joshua's distinguished career. The numbers themselves are daunting, but in addition, there were the chariots, against which Israel had never before fought. Josephus says, "This host of enemies dismayed both Joshua himself and the Israelites, and in the excess of their fear they scarce durst hope for success."[1]

The Bible does not say that Joshua was made fearful by the size and nature of the opposing forces, but it is possible that he was, since God intervened again to promise him success. "Do not be afraid of them, because by this time tomorrow I will hand all of them over to Israel, slain. You are to hamstring their horses and burn their chariots" (Joshua 11:6).

If Joshua was intimidated by the size of the army, he refused to show it. The story says that he immediately marched against these enemies and fell on them suddenly, just as he had marched against the southern coalition at Gibeon and routed it. This battle was probably the most violent and bloody of the entire conquest, although very few details are given. All we are told is that "the LORD gave them into the hand of Israel" and that "they defeated

---

1. Josephus, *Jewish Antiquities,* books V-VIII, H. St. J. Thackeray and Ralph Marcus, trans. (Cambridge: Harvard University Press, 1958), p. 31.

them and pursued them all the way to Greater Sidon, to Misrephoth Maim, and to the Valley of Mizpah on the east, until no survivors were left. Joshua did to them as the LORD had directed: He hamstrung their horses and burned their chariots'' (Joshua 11:8, 9).

After the defeat and destruction of the northern coalition, Joshua turned on the cities, beginning with Hazor, which had headed the coalition. At this point we are not given the names of the cities Joshua conquered. That comes later, in chapter twelve. Instead, we are told that Joshua took the "entire land." The description that follows covers the *entire* conquest, not merely the northern campaign. The text describes six areas:

1. The hill country, part of which was to the south and part of which was to the north.
2. The Negev, the increasingly poorer land stretching south from Judah.
3. Goshen, an area farther south, the exact location of which has not been determined (not the place in Egypt where the Jews settled in the days of Joseph).
4. The western foothills, the region stretching down toward the Mediterranean Sea.
5. The Arabah, the fertile land east of the Jordan River.
6. The mountains of Israel with their foothills, which includes everything to the north.

The territory thus conquered and occupied is extensive. It stretches from Sidon to Egypt and from the Mediterranean Sea to the desert. It was, indeed, all the land that had been promised to Israel.

Summary of the Conquest

The book of Joshua is divided into two parts: the conquest and the settlement of the land. The conquest story ends with chapter 12, so it is appropriate that chapter 12 is a summary of the conquest. It goes back to the battles fought under Moses on the far side of the Jordan before the invasion of the land. The territory conquered then was the portion given to the descendants of Reuben, Gad, and the half tribe of Manasseh. Then the victories under Joshua are summarized, concluding with a list of the kings who were defeated and killed. It is something of a checklist:

the king of Jericho	one
the king of Ai (near Bethel)	one
the king of Jerusalem	one
the king of Hebron	one
the king of Jarmuth	one
the king of Lachish	one . . . .

The list continues that way for thirty-one items and concludes, ". . . thirty-one kings in all" (Joshua 12:9–24).

So ended the official conquest of the land of Canaan under the command of Joshua the son of Nun.

Qualities of Leadership

The presence of Joshua is felt throughout the rest of the book that bears his name. In fact, the book ends with his great sermons to the leaders and people, in which he challenges them to choose God and serve him faithfully. Still, this is a good place to look back over this great general's victories and ask about the qualities that made him such an exceptional leader. I see six of them.

Joshua did not let short-term gains deter him from long-range objectives. Joshua could have done this. The chief illustration is the discovery of the hiding place of the kings of the southern coalition during the running battle below Gibeon. The discovery of these kings was a great good turn of fortune, most certainly given to Joshua by God. To have killed them would have been a great advantage. Nevertheless, Joshua realized that his chief task was the defeat of their armies and the occupation of the southern lands, so he had the cave in which the kings were hiding sealed up and dealt with them later.

Most Christians can learn from Joshua at this point, since we all are often confronted with good but short-range opportunities, and these frequently turn us aside from our chief tasks.

Some years ago I was talking with Lorne Saney, the former head of the Navigators. He told me how he manages to keep his priorities straight in the midst of a very pressured life-style. Each year, after Christmas, he takes time out to set his personal objectives for the year. He writes them down and prioritizes them, determining how he is going to achieve each during the next twelve months. He does this quarterly, which allows him to review and revise, seeing how far he has come or how his thinking may have changed. The thing that impressed me most in this conversation was Saney's description of doing the same thing each Sunday night in preparation for the new week's work. As he does this, he prays about it. Then he tries to follow through, doing the things of greatest importance first. Something like this would be helpful to many distracted and disoriented Christians.

Joshua understood the need others have for visible encouragement. When Joshua returned to deal with the captured kings, he did not put them to death at once. Instead, he called his commanders forward and had them pass by him, putting their feet on the necks of the kings who had been made to prostrate themselves before him in the dust. Joshua encouraged his leaders, saying essentially what God had said to encourage him, "Do not be afraid; do not be discouraged. Be strong and courageous. This is what the LORD will do to all the enemies you are going to fight" (Joshua 10:25). Joshua knew there would be many long and difficult battles ahead, and he saw that his commanders needed regular and dramatic encouragement to persevere.

So, too, today. One of the most giving churches (in proportion to its membership) in America is the Ward Presbyterian Church of Livonia, Michigan, pastored by Dr. Bartlett Hess. The people of that church give over two million dollars to Christian work each year. How do they do it? Hess explains that the secret is encouragement.[2] Some pastors are constantly browbeating their congregations because they do not give enough money. Hess compliments them on what they are giving and gives careful regular reports of what their gifts are accomplishing. The same principles hold for raising children; they need to be encouraged. It also holds for relationships between husbands and wives, employers and employees, and others.

Joshua took no shortcuts, but pursued the campaign in a logical, step-by-step progression. Even today, students of Scripture are impressed with this man's consistent and logical pursuit of the conquest. He defeated the kings and their armies. Then he proceeded step-by-step against the fortified towns. There was no other way to conquer the land completely. The progressive overthrowing of these cities, which is described so briefly in Joshua 10–12, took seven years.

It would help many of us to be as consistent as Joshua in our living of the Christian life. In our day we are bombarded with books, talks, and seminars that are supposed to give us shortcuts to spiritual growth and maturity. We waste much time with these, since there are no shortcuts in the development of the Christian life. There is no mystery. The Bible tells us that we are to read and study the Bible, pray, worship together with others of God's people, witness to non-Christians, and serve others in specific

2. Bartlett L. and Margaret Johnston Hess, *How to Have a Giving Church* (Nashville and New York: Abingdon Press, 1974).

ways. This is what works and has always worked, but it is no shortcut to maturity. It is just something we must do and continue to do throughout our lives as Christian people. Joshua is a model for us in this area.

Joshua did not allow his early errors to unsettle or defeat him. Joshua was a great leader, and God used him greatly. But this does not mean that Joshua was perfect. We are told of two mistakes made early in his campaigns. First, he attacked Ai on the advice of his spies without consulting the Lord, and so suffered an ignominious defeat. There was sin in the camp. But he would have been told of this and could have dealt with it, if he had consulted God first. Second, he was taken in by the ruse of the Gibeonites for the same reason. He made a decision on the basis of his observations and did not pray.

I suppose the devil came to Joshua many times after that, as he so often comes to us, and accused him of being a great failure and therefore useless to God. This is one of the devil's tricks. He will say, "Well, you certainly messed up on that. You've disgraced yourself and made yourself useless, as far as serving God is concerned. You might as well give up. Forget God. Serve me." Joshua was not taken in by that, and neither should we be. He recognized his failure as a failure, but he confessed it and put it behind him. He did what the apostle Paul told the Philippians he did: ". . . Forgetting what is behind and straining toward what is ahead, I press on toward the goal to win the prize for which God has called me heavenward in Christ Jesus" (Philippians 3:13, 14).

Joshua believed God implicitly. Theologian R. C. Sproul points out that there is a great difference between believing in God and believing God. Many people will say that they believe in God; that is, they admit that he exists. But they do not believe *him;* they do not believe what he says. Joshua believed God and,

like all heroes of the faith, acted on that belief. God told him, ". . . Be strong and courageous. Do not be terrified; do not be discouraged, for the LORD your God will be with you wherever you go" (Joshua 1:9). Joshua firmly expected God to defeat his enemies. So he attacked them anticipating victory.

Joshua obeyed completely.   In my opinion the most important thing that is said about Joshua in this book is found in Joshua 11:15: "As the LORD commanded his servant Moses, so Moses commanded Joshua, and Joshua did it; he left nothing undone of all that the LORD commanded Moses." What a remarkable statement! Joshua "left nothing undone of all that the LORD had commanded Moses." He was told to conquer Canaan, so he did it step-by-step in obedience to God's commands. First Jericho, then Ai, then Gibeon, then the cities of the south, then the cities of the north. Then he arranged the settlement described in Joshua 13–22. He did it all. No one could point to one single thing and say, "Joshua, you forgot to do this. The task isn't finished."

How great it would be if that could be the case with each of us—if no one could point to anything we had left undone, but instead could say, "John Smith has left nothing undone of all that the Lord commanded." If that were the case, we would all see conquests even more extensive and blessing even greater than those experienced by the armies of Israel.

Chapter Twelve

Dividing the Land
Joshua 13:1–19:51

> *When Joshua was old and well advanced in years, the*
> *LORD said to him, "You are very old, and there are still*
> *very large areas of land to be taken over. . . . Be sure to*
> *allocate this land to Israel for an inheritance, as I have*
> *instructed you, and divide it as an inheritance among the*
> *nine tribes and half of the tribe of Manasseh. . . .*
> *And so they finished dividing the land.*
>
> Joshua 13:1, 6, 7; 19:51

There are two main parts to the book of Joshua: chapters 1–12, which describe the conquest of Canaan, and chapters 13–24, which describe the division of the land. We are at the beginning of chapter 13, so we are now exactly halfway through the book and at the start of the second section.

A number of years have passed. A quick reading of the campaigns described in Joshua 10–12 might give the impression that the defeat of the city fortresses of the north and south was accomplished in a short while, but that would be wrong. It is true that the great battles of the conquest occurred in rapid succession and the strength of the Canaanites was broken in a matter of weeks or months. But that was only the beginning. Joshua had defeated the combined armies of the Canaanites in two great battles at Gibeon and by the Waters of Merom, but these were followed by the necessary subjugation of the city fortresses, and that took time.

How long did it take? Well, in Joshua 14:7 we are told that Caleb was forty years old when Moses sent him to spy out the land. He was eighty-five when the war was over and he was about to receive his inheritance (v. 10). The difference is forty-five years, thirty-eight of which were spent in the desert with the people of Israel before the beginning of the conquest. So the wars of conquest must have taken approximately seven years.

The second half of this book begins by saying that Joshua was old. We do not know exactly how old he was, but he was probably Caleb's senior. And at any rate, when he dies, at the end of the book, Joshua is one hundred and ten. Most commentators believe that he was probably nearly ninety at this point. The problem at this time was that although the great fortresses of the land (with a few exceptions, like Jerusalem) had been overthrown, there were still hundreds of smaller towns or Canaanite enclaves still to be taken. What was to be done about these? The plan the Lord gave Joshua, and which he executed, was to divide the land among the Jewish tribes and then send each to settle its own portion by subduing the Canaanites still in it.

The key to Joshua 13–19 is in the opening verse of the section: ". . . There are still very large areas of land to be taken over" (Joshua 13:1). The task of doing this was now assigned to each of the tribes.

The First Division

Even this was done deliberately in two stages. The first stage of this division and settlement is in Joshua 13–17. It concerns the two and a half tribes settled east of the Jordan (Reuben, Gad, and half the tribe of Manasseh); Judah, which was settled in the south; and Ephraim and the other half of the tribe of Manasseh, which were settled in the north. This seems to have been done with military concerns in mind. The north, south, and east were Israel's military frontiers, so by settling five strong tribes in these areas, Joshua created a secure environment for the rest of the tribes.

Reuben, Gad, and half the tribe of Manasseh (Joshua 13:8–33). The allocation of land to the tribes of Reuben, Gad, and half the tribe of Manasseh was not new, since it had been determined by Moses before the conquest. These people had requested this land, and Moses had granted it on the condition that they would not use the inheritance to avoid their share of the conquest but would join with the other tribes in the battles necessary to secure Canaan (*see* Numbers 32; Deuteronomy 3:18–20; Joshua 1:12–15). The record of the assigning of the trans-Jordanian territory to these people is included here because this is the section of the book in which the overall apportionment of the land is recorded.

Judah (Joshua 15:1–63). The distribution of the southern portions of the country to Judah occupies the entire fifteenth chapter and is quite important, because Judah had become the most important of the tribes. The patriarch of this tribe, Judah, was the fourth of Jacob's twelve sons, born after Reuben, Simeon, and Levi. He would not normally have been given prominence, were it not for the sins of his older brothers that disqualified them from the special blessings of the firstborn. Reuben had dishonored his father by sleeping with his father's concubine Bilhah (Genesis 35:22). Simeon and Levi had led the massacre against the Shechemites, which Jacob said had made his name a ''stench'' in the land (Genesis 34).

The full blessing of the firstborn (forfeited by Reuben, Simeon, and Levi) did not go to Judah. A portion of it went to Joseph in the persons of his two sons, Ephraim and Manasseh (1 Chronicles 5:1, 2). That is, Joseph received a double portion of his father's inheritance by means of each of his sons becoming father to a Jewish tribe and receiving a separate tribal territory.

Nevertheless, Judah was given the right of rule. According to the prophecy of his father, recorded in Genesis 49:8–12, Judah was to give birth to kings and eventually to the King of kings, the Messiah.

What a list of kings this was!

David, the greatest of all Israel's kings, was described as being "a man after God's own heart." He ruled for forty years, brought peace to Israel, and was the author of many of her most beautiful psalms.

Solomon was noted for his wisdom. It was during his reign that Israel rose to the pinnacle of her glory. He constructed the great temple in Jerusalem and was the author of Proverbs, Ecclesiastes, and the Song of Songs.

Much later, Josiah was used by God to bring about a revival of religion in which the law was rediscovered, the temple purified, and centers of the worship of false gods destroyed throughout the land.

These kings reigned in Jerusalem, which was on Judah's northern border. The Jews were unable to take Jerusalem at the time of the conquest, which we are told in Joshua 15:63, but they were finally driven out by David, as recorded in 2 Samuel 5:6, 7.

Ephraim and the other half tribe of Manasseh (Joshua 16:1–17:18). An interesting feature of this allocation is that a major portion was given to the five daughters of Zelophehad: Mahlah, Noah, Hoglah, Milcah, and Tirzah (Joshua 17:3–6). Usually land was left to sons. But Zelophehad had died without having had sons, and the daughters of this man had approached Moses, saying, "Why should our father's name disappear from his clan because he had no son? Give us property among our father's relatives" (Numbers 27:4; *see* Numbers 27:1–11; 36:1–12). God told Moses that the women's appeal was right, so Joshua 17 records them receiving their inheritance.

The interesting thing about these early apportionments of land, as Francis Schaeffer points out, is that they were according to decisions or principles previously recorded in the writings of Moses. So again we are reminded that the people had a written Word of God that they considered binding. "The Pentateuch was already completely normative. It was the Word of God to these people." In the case of Zelophehad's daughters, the women appealed to the writings of Moses as to something "which not only conveyed some sort of religious feeling but also gave specific commands which were to be obeyed in detail."[1]

Division by Lot at Shiloh

Toward the end of this period, Israel's camp was moved from Gilgal to Shiloh, which was in the high country between Ai and Gerazim. It was probably changed for military reasons, since the frontiers of the nation were now secured. Here the second stage of the division took place. A survey was done, the remaining territory was divided into seven portions, and a careful description of each portion (a land title deed) was written down. Then the remaining tribes were assigned their portions by the casting of lots, which means the choice was God's.

Benjamin (Joshua 18:11–28).   The first lot was Benjamin's. This relatively small tribe received a portion of territory lying between Ephraim and Judah (Joseph's portion) (Joshua 18:11). It was not a large tract of land, as befitted Benjamin's small size, but it included important places: Jericho, Ai, Bethel, Gibeon, and others. Most importantly, it lay close to Judah, touching Judah's territory at Jerusalem. In later years, when the nation divided into the northern kingdom of Israel and the southern kingdom of Judah, Benjamin remained with Judah in the south and so preserved the true worship of God for a time.

1. Francis A. Schaeffer, *Joshua and the Flow of Biblical History* (Downers Grove, Ill.: InterVarsity Press, 1975), pp. 164, 171.

Simeon (Joshua 19:1–9). Simeon and Levi were the patriarchs who had led the slaughter against the Shechemites, and in Jacob's prophecy regarding his sons' future, recorded in Genesis 49, they are judged by being kept from possession of territory in the conquered land. Jacob's words were: ". . . I will scatter them in Jacob and disperse them in Israel" (Genesis 49:7). This was fulfilled, though in a most gracious way. True, Simeon did not receive his own territory, but he was allocated land within the land of Judah. Levi received no tribal allotment. Levi was literally scattered throughout the territory of the other tribes. But the Levites were made priests, and thus their scattering was actually turned into a blessing for the other tribes and for themselves. They were settled in forty-eight priestly cities, where they were to represent and teach about the true God of Israel.

Zebulun (Joshua 19:10–16). Four of the smaller Jewish tribes were settled to the north, even above the territory assigned to Ephraim and the two halves of the tribe of Manasseh. Zebulun was north of the plain of Megiddo, almost directly east of Mount Carmel.

Issachar (Joshua 19:17–23). Issachar was Zebulun's brother, both having been born of Jacob's first wife, Leah. They were the ninth and tenth of Jacob's twelve sons and, being younger, had probably grown up together and had become quite close. Therefore, in the distribution of the land, their territories lay next to each other. Issachar touched Zebulun on the eastern side and was also north of Manasseh.

Asher (Joshua 19:24–31). The land given to Asher extended up the Mediterranean coast from Mount Carmel to Sidon in the north. It was extremely fertile country, but it was also exposed to the corrupting influences of the Gentile cities of the region, particularly Tyre and Sidon.

Naphtali (Joshua 19:32–39). The territory of Naphtali ran parallel to that of Asher, but it was inland. It included the important New Testament cities of Capernaum, Cana, and Bethsaida, although these did not exist at the time of the conquest. Isaiah introduced his prophecy of the Messiah by a blessing upon Naphtali and Zebulun, which were to be called "Galilee of the Gentiles" at that time. He wrote, ". . . In the past he [God] humbled the land of Zebulun and the land of Naphtali, but in the future he will honor Galilee of the Gentiles, by the way of the sea, along the Jordan—the people walking in darkness have seen a great light . . ." (Isaiah 9:1, 2).

Dan (Joshua 19:40–48). The last of the tribes to receive land was Dan. Dan's territory was farther south, in the area between the sea and Jerusalem. This was Philistine territory, including (among other settlements) the great cities of Aijalon, Ekron, and Gath. It is significant that Joshua 19 records that the people of Dan had trouble taking possession of this territory. (We know that the Philistines remained there to plague Israel in later years.) Instead they attacked the city of Leshem, subdued it, and occupied its territory.

At the very end of this account we are told that after Joshua had finished dividing the land into its allotted portions, the Israelites gave him his own inheritance. He had asked for and now received the hill town of Timnath Serah in the territory of Ephraim, which was appropriate, since he was of the tribe of Ephraim (see Numbers 13:8). This portion of the book concludes by saying, "These are the territories that Eleazar the priest, Joshua son of Nun and the heads of the tribal clans of Israel assigned by lot at Shiloh in the presence of the LORD at the entrance to the Tent of Meeting. And so they finished dividing the land'' (Joshua 19:51). This is a satisfying end to a great military and spiritual adventure.

Possessing Our Possessions

In the last chapter we looked at some of the outstanding characteristics of Joshua, but it is worth saying at this point, by way of summary and emphasis, that the outstanding characteristic of this great man was his faithfulness in service to God and God's people to the very end. Ninety years old is pretty old. Many people stop any kind of service to God long before that age, and many others (even though, at a younger age, they are still working) are not very faithful in their work. Not Joshua! Joshua had been given an assignment to conquer and possess Canaan, and he did not quit until that great assignment was completed. In this respect, it is significant that he did not receive his own portion of the land until he had done everything he could to destroy the Canaanite strongholds.

Joshua's faithfulness to his task did not mean that the people had nothing to do or that the need for faithfulness on their part was less important. By dividing the land and dispatching the various tribes to possess it, Joshua acknowledged the people's own responsibility and encouraged them in it.

This is important to see, because Christians often regard a strong leader as an excuse for their own lack of achievement. If another is working, they sit back and enjoy the benefits of his or her accomplishment. This is not right. It is true that God apportions gifts irregularly. In Christ's parables of the talents, one servant received five talents of money, another two, and a third just one (Matthew 25:14–30; *see* a variation of this parable in Luke 19:11–27). But the point of these parables is that each servant was responsible for using the talent given to him. The one who refused to use his talent, even though he had only one, was judged severely.

As Christian people we, too, like the Israelites, must possess our possessions. The idea of possessing what has already been given to us by God is a theme many commentators on Joshua develop, particularly those who treat the book as an allegory of the Christian life.[2] They point out, quite rightly, that just as the Jewish people had been given Canaan but nevertheless needed to possess it mile by mile and person by person, Christians have been given an inheritance that likewise must be possessed through individual attainment. These commentators speak of knowledge, holiness, and the gifts of the Holy Spirit. Clearly these are all ours. But we enter into them only to the extent that we come to understand and appropriate the Bible, draw close to and obey the Lord Jesus Christ, and actually serve others with the gifts we are given.

I apply this in yet another way. In Revelation 11:15, one of the angels of God sounds a trumpet and the hosts of heaven cry out: ''The kingdom of the world has become the kingdom of our Lord and of his Christ, and he will reign for ever and ever.'' That verse is an actualization of something that has already taken place in principle and involves each of Christ's followers. In God's eyes, the world and its kingdoms have already been given to Jesus, and it is on the basis of this possession and the accompanying authority of Jesus over the world that his disciples are sent into the world to call its people and kingdoms to obedience (*see* Matthew 28:18–20). In other words, we are sent into the world to announce Christ's rule, bring people to him, and thus actualize his possession. Evangelism is part of what theologians call our ''cultural mandate.''

---

2. F. B. Meyer, *Joshua and the Land of Promise* (Fort Washington, Pa.: Christian Literature Crusade, 1977), pp. 150–158; Alan Redpath, *Victorious Christian Living: Studies in the Book of Joshua* (Westwood, N. J.: Fleming H. Revell Co., 1955), pp. 170–181, are two chief examples. *See* my discussion of these approaches in chapter one.

Although there is land for every Christian to possess, each must be possessed by Christ before he or she can possess it, for it is by his strength and not by our own that we can do anything. The kingdoms of this world are our inheritance, for they are Christ's, and Christ is ours. But we are Christ's inheritance—he spoke of us to the Father as "those whom you gave me"—and we must be fully possessed by him if we are to enter into all that Christ has for us.

Chapter Thirteen

That Magnificent Old Man
Joshua 14:6–15

Now the men of Judah approached Joshua at Gilgal, and Caleb son of Jephunneh the Kenizzite said to him, "You know what the LORD said to Moses the man of God at Kadesh Barnea about you and me. I was forty years old when Moses the servant of the LORD sent me from Kadesh Barnea to explore the land. And I brought him back a report according to my convictions, but my brothers who went up with me made the hearts of the people melt with fear. I, however, followed the LORD my God wholeheartedly. So on that day Moses swore to me, 'The land on which your feet have walked will be your inheritance and that of your children forever, because you have followed the LORD my God wholeheartedly.'

"Now then, just as the LORD promised, he has kept me alive for forty-five years since the time he said this to Moses, while Israel moved about in the desert. So here I am today, eighty-five years old! I am still as strong today as the day Moses sent me out; I'm just as vigorous to go out to battle now as I was then. Now give me this hill country that the LORD promised me that day. You yourself heard then that the Anakites were there and their cities were large and fortified, but, the LORD helping me, I will drive them out just as he said."

138

> *Then Joshua blessed Caleb son of Jephunneh and gave*
> *him Hebron as his inheritance. So Hebron has belonged*
> *to Caleb son of Jephunneh the Kenizzite ever since,*
> *because he followed the* LORD, *the God of Israel,*
> *wholeheartedly. . . .*
> *Then the land had rest from war.*
>
> Joshua 14:6–15

In the presence of a very great man, other people are often overshadowed. It is not that the overshadowed men are not often great themselves, perhaps even greater in some ways than those who command attention. But for various reasons, certain leaders just shine out, and other leaders are neglected. It was like this with Joshua and Moses. So it was again with Caleb in the presence of his companion Joshua.

It is a pity that this should have been true for Caleb, for he was an extraordinary man. We are not told much about him. Joshua would have been overlooked far more than he is if it were not for the book that bears his name. Caleb does not even have a book. He is mentioned in only a half dozen or a dozen places in the Bible, only three of them in Joshua (Joshua 14:6–15; 15:13–19; 21:12). Although we may forget him, Caleb was not forgotten by God or his people. Caleb fought side by side with Joshua for the many long years of the conquest, and when the fighting was nearly over and it came time to divide the land for settlement, Caleb was given a portion that had been promised to him many decades before. Thus God honored him, and the people honored him as well.

A Distinguished History

The first time we meet Caleb is in Numbers 13, the chapter that tells of Moses' selection of the twelve spies who were to cross the Jordan and search out the land. This was two years after the people had come out of Egypt, and Caleb was forty years old at the time.

In the listing of the spies in Numbers 13:4–15, Caleb is cited as a representative of the tribe of Judah, which means he was a member of that tribe. But elsewhere he is described as being the son of Jephunneh the Kenizzite (Joshua 14:6, 14), and Kenizzites were not Jews. They were people who lived in the land being conquered. In fact, they are mentioned in the original promise of the land to Abraham, recorded in Genesis 15:18–21. ". . . To your descendants I give this land, from the river of Egypt to the great river, the Euphrates—the land of the Kenites, *Kenizzites,* Kadmonites, Hittites, Perizzites, Rephaites, Amorites, Canaanites, Girgashites and Jebusites."

So Caleb was a foreigner, or at least his father was. We do not know how he came to be in Egypt with the Jewish people. Perhaps he was thrown together with them during their years of slavery under the Pharaohs, or maybe his ancestors went down with the Jews originally. At any rate, at some point Caleb's father obviously identified with the Jews and was loyal to that new association. So was Caleb. In fact, one of his chief characteristics was faithfulness. So although he was a foreigner, he nevertheless regarded himself as a faithful follower of the Jews' God and followed him to the very end of his life.

The thirteenth chapter of Numbers does not tell much about how the twelve spies explored the land, only that "they went up and explored the land from the Desert of Zin as far as Rehob, toward Lebo Hamath. They went up through the Negev and came to Hebron, where Ahiman, Sheshai and Talmai, the descendants of Anak, lived" (vv. 21, 22). However, I suspect that from the beginning Caleb had a special interest in Hebron, the only city that is actually described in detail. I think he insisted on the spies going there or they split up and he chose to spy out Hebron himself.

Why? Hebron had played an important role in the life of the Jewish patriarchs, and Caleb, as a new member of the nation, would have wanted to see where the roots of his new allegiances lay.

Hebron was the place at which Sarah, Abraham's wife, had died and where Abraham had purchased a field containing the cave of Machpelah, which he used as Sarah's tomb. It was the only piece of Canaan that Abraham actually owned in his lifetime, the Jews' toehold in Canaan, as it were. Here Abraham himself was buried, and later Isaac and Rebekah, Jacob, and eventually Joseph, who had commanded that his bones be brought up out of Egypt and buried there when the Jews left Egypt and conquered Canaan. Hebron was the closest thing in Canaan to a sacred Jewish site. It was probably for this reason that Caleb, the new Jewish citizen, insisted on seeing it and later claimed it as his special inheritance. '

The Descendants of Anak

There was something else about Hebron that Caleb and the other spies saw, though they reacted to it differently. Hebron was the home of giants. The spies who saw that the land was good but did not believe they were able to conquer it said:

> . . . "We went into the land to which you sent us, and it does flow with milk and honey! Here is its fruit. But the people who live there are powerful, and the cities are fortified and very large. We even saw descendants of Anak there. . . . The land we explored devours those living in it. All the people we saw there are of great size. We saw the Nephilim there (the descendants of Anak come from the Nephilim). We seemed like grasshoppers in our own eyes, and we looked the same to them.
> Numbers 13:27, 28, 32, 33

This was an exaggeration, of course. All the people of the land were not giants. But the spies had seen something that had frightened them. The Nephilim were giants (this is the word used of the "heroes of old, men of renown" in Genesis 6:4); Anak was a descendant of the Nephilim, and three of Anak's descendants lived in Hebron. Numbers 13:22 even names them: Ahiman, Sheshai, and Talmai. Ten spies saw these giants and concluded that they themselves were like grasshoppers. Only Caleb and Joshua believed that the land could be conquered. Caleb said, ". . . 'We should go up and take possession of the land, for we can certainly do it' '' (Numbers 13:30).

We know what happened. The people listened to the timid majority, as people generally will, and God judged their unbelief by condemning that entire generation to wander in the desert until all those forty years of age or over, with the exception of Joshua and Caleb, had died. But something of that brief glimpse of Hebron during the spying operation stuck with Caleb, and he never seemed able to get it out of his mind. Many times he must have said to himself, "When we finally do get back into Canaan, that is the place I am going to have for myself. I said that God could drive out the giants, and with God's help, that is precisely what I am going to do."

After the initial spying operation, Caleb asked Moses to grant him the hill country containing Hebron, and Moses had consented. Now, toward the end of the conquest, Caleb said to Joshua, "Give me this hill country that the Lord promised me that day. You yourself heard then that the Anakites were there and their cities were large and fortified, but, the Lord helping me, I will drive them out just as he said" (Joshua 14:12).

This was Caleb's vision during the thirty-eight years of desert wandering and the seven years of the conquest. F. B. Meyer says:

> Amid the marchings and counter-marchings, the innumerable deaths, the murmurings and rebellions of the people, he retained a steadfast purpose to do only God's will, to please him, to know no other leader, and to heed no other voice. It was of no use to try and involve that stout lion's cub in any movement against Moses and Aaron. He would be no party to Miriam's jealous spite. He would not be allured by the wiles of the girls of Moab. Always strong and true and pure and noble; like a rock in a

changeful sea, like a snowcapped peak in a change of cloud and storm and sun. A man in whose strong nature weaker men could hide, and who must have been a tower of strength to that new and young generation which grew up to fill the vacant places in the van of Israel. The Nestor of the Hebrew camp, in him the words of the Psalmist were anticipated, that he bore fruit in his old age, and to the last was fat and flourishing.[1]

The character of a lifetime at last bore fruit in the abundant service of this magnificent man.

A Great but Simple Man

What was the secret of Caleb's greatness? It is not difficult to answer that question: Caleb had total faith in God, and he utterly gave himself to God.

Great men are never really complicated. The complicated people are the weak ones, beset by dozens of conflicting causes and motives, never quite knowing how to get it all together. They see one side of an issue, but they also see the other side. They see the advantage of one course of action, but they recognize that it might be better to do something else. Great men are not like this. They are not naive. They know that issues are sometimes complicated and that there are often different paths that can be taken, but they see the important cause and the best path and then follow it consistently.

Athanasius had this kind of greatness. He perceived the importance to Christianity of preserving the full deity of Jesus Christ and so fought for that understanding through an entire lifetime of theological controversy. In the end, he was vindicated.

Luther was another such man. He seized upon the doctrine of justification by faith and stood for it faithfully, even at the risk of his life. He was vindicated.

1. F. B. Meyer, *Joshua and the Land of Promise* (Fort Washington, Pa.: Christian Literature Crusade, 1977), p. 161.

Wilberforce was great in these terms, also. He knew the complexities of the slavery issue, but he also knew that slavery was wrong and so fought until it was driven from the British Empire.

Lincoln fought on for the same cause in the great war between the states.

The list could be multiplied many times over, but the point I am making is that Caleb had this kind of greatness. He was great because he had total faith in God and gave himself utterly to God.

Why did Caleb have such faith in God? Again the answer is simple: because he had his eyes on God, and not on the vacillating or terrifying things around him. This is the significance of that almost humorous report of the ten spies recorded in Numbers 13 and its contrast with the report of Caleb and Joshua. Not one of the spies disagreed on the value of the land of Canaan. It was indeed a land "flowing with milk and honey," as God said. Nor did they differ on their description of the people and their cities. The cities *were* large and well fortified. The people *were* numerous, and there *were* giants in the land. The point at which they differed was in their awareness of God. The ten looked at themselves and the giants and concluded that a conquest of those people was impossible. Compared to the giants, the Jews seemed like grasshoppers. Caleb and Joshua looked at God rather than circumstances, and when compared to God, the giants were grasshoppers. That is why they said, ". . . Do not be afraid of the people of the land, because we will swallow them up. Their protection is gone, but the Lord is with us. Do not be afraid of them" (Numbers 14:9).

Alan Redpath wrote of Caleb and Joshua's faith: "The majority measured the giants against their own strength; Caleb and Joshua measured the giants against God. The majority trembled; the two triumphed. The majority had great giants but a little God. Caleb had a great God and little giants."[2]

---

2. Alan Redpath, *Victorious Christian Living: Studies in the Book of Joshua* (Westwood, N.J.: Fleming H. Revell Co., 1955), pp. 197, 198.

There's another illustration of this principle. Peter, one of the Lord's disciples, once saw Jesus walking toward him on the Sea of Galilee. Peter was in a boat at the time, and the weather was stormy. But in a burst of faith, he called out, "Lord, if it's you, . . . tell me to come to you on the water" (Matthew 14:28). When Jesus bid him come, Peter got out of the boat and began to walk over the water toward Jesus.

Alas, he took his eyes off Jesus and looked at the waves instead. When he did, he began to sink, and Christ had to reach out to save him. As long as Peter kept his eyes on Jesus, the waves were not terrifying. He would have said, as Caleb did, ". . . We [I] can certainly do it" (Numbers 13:30). But when he looked at the waves, they became overpowering and he seemed to be a very small thing about to be engulfed by them.

"How big is your God?" asked J. B. Phillips.[3] Caleb had a big God, and Caleb's big God did mighty things for Caleb.

Heart Service

There is also another part to Caleb's great spiritual strength: Caleb gave himself up to God utterly. This is what comes out most forcefully in Joshua 14. The key word is *wholeheartedly:* ". . . The land on which your feet have walked will be your inheritance and that of your children forever, because you have followed the LORD my God *wholeheartedly*" (Joshua 14:9, emphasis mine); "So Hebron has belonged to Caleb son of Jephunnek the Kennizzite ever since, because he followed the LORD the God of Israel, *wholeheartedly* (Joshua 14:14, emphasis mine).

Wholeheartedly means with all your heart. It is the idea embodied in what Jesus called the first and greatest of the commandments: "Love the Lord your God with all your heart and with all

3. J. B. Phillips, *Your God Is Too Small* (New York: The Macmillan Company, 1967).

your soul and with all your mind'' (Matthew 22:37; see Deuteronomy 6:5). Nothing could be more basic to true discipleship. Yet how many of us do this or even worry about not doing it? Caleb, although he was certainly a sinner like the rest of us, could say that this is what had characterized his many years of service.

And he was still doing it at the end! Isn't that remarkable? Caleb had served God for forty-five years, and he was now eighty-five years old—a good time for anyone to retire, and twenty years past the retirement age of most. But Caleb was not finished yet. He had fought with Joshua through the seven long years of the campaign. He had earned many laurels. But now he wanted to climax his distinguished career with a victory over the area of the country he had seen and claimed four and a half decades earlier. And he did it! Joshua 15 tells us that the country given to Caleb had two main cities: Hebron and Debir. Caleb himself took Hebron, driving out the three descendants of Anak: Sheshai, Ahiman, and Talmai. Then he offered his daughter to the man who could take Debir. Othniel, the son of Caleb's brother, took it. So Othniel and Caleb's daughter Acsah were married and settled in their own portion of the land.

Looking to Jesus

I cannot close this chapter without noting that in his wholeheartedly giving of himself to God, Caleb contrasts with most of the other people of Israel during this period. Caleb was given Hebron and took it, driving the Anakites from the land. Sadly, this was not true of the majority of the nation. Again and again in this section we are told that they did not entirely drive out the Canaanites. The land was theirs, the power of the Canaanites was broken, but they did not fully possess the possessions God had given to them.

Why was this? Again there is a simple answer: They did not serve the Lord wholeheartedly, as Caleb did. I think they were probably tired of fighting and just wanted a little peace for a while. They wanted to enjoy the spoils of their battles. Their religion was becoming similar to that urged on so many professing Christians today. They wanted to be "saved, safe, and satisfied." Well, saved they may well have been, and safe, too. But they should not have been satisfied to the extent of abandoning their commission. There were ". . . still very large areas of land to be taken over" (Joshua 13:1), and they were not to settle down in peace and prosperity until they were.

There are other things besides giants that can get our eyes off God and his service. We can get our eyes on peace, comfort, or a thousand other things that wrongly compete for God's place.

Do you remember those verses that come immediately after that great chapter on the heroes of the faith in Hebrews? Hebrews 11 lists many of the magnificent men and women of the Old Testament, those who contended for the faith and triumphed. We are inspired by such examples, and rightly so. But immediately after their stories have been told, the author of the book applies their examples of faith to us, saying:

> Therefore, since we are surrounded by such a great cloud of witnesses, let us throw off everything that hinders and the sin that so easily entangles, and let us run with perseverance the race marked out for us. Let us fix our eyes on Jesus, the author and perfecter of our faith, who for the joy set before him endured the cross, scorning its shame, and sat down at the right hand of the throne of God. Consider him who endured such opposition from sinful men, so that you will not grow weary and lose heart.
>
> Hebrews 12:1–3

I am sure there were times when Caleb was quite weary, but he did not lose heart; he had his eyes set on God, who was giving him the victory. No more will we lose heart, if our eyes are fixed on our great Savior and Lord, Jesus Christ.

Chapter Fourteen

The Special Cities
Joshua 20:1–21:45

Then the Lord *said to Joshua: "Tell the Israelites to designate the cities of refuge, as I instructed you through Moses, so that anyone who kills a person accidentally and unintentionally may flee there and find protection from the avenger of blood.*

"When he flees to one of these cities, he is to stand in the entrance of the city gate and state his case before the elders of that city. Then they are to admit him into their city and give him a place to live with them. If the avenger of blood pursues him, they must not surrender the one accused, because he killed his neighbor unintentionally and without malice aforethought. He is to stay in that city until he has stood trial before the assembly and until the death of the high priest who is serving at that time. Then he may go back to his own home in the town from which he fled.

Joshua 20:1–6

Now the family heads of the Levites approached Eleazar the priest, Joshua son of Nun, and the heads of the other tribal families of Israel at Shiloh in Canaan and said to them, "The Lord *commanded through Moses that you give us towns to live in, with pasturelands for our livestock." So, as the* Lord *had commanded, the Israel-*

ites gave the Levites the following towns and pasture-
lands out of their own inheritance.

Joshua 21:1–3

Most people have some pride in the city in which they grew up, which is a way of saying that from the point of view of the native, every city, like every person, is special. I grew up in McKeesport, Pennsylvania, a mill town at the juncture of the Monongahela and Youghogheny rivers in the western part of the state. Maybe there was not a whole lot to be proud of there, but we were proud of our high school football team. We reminded people that Shirley Jones, the actress, had come from our part of the country. We were just upriver from Pittsburgh, which did not help a whole lot, either, except that someone had written a popular song that went, "There's a pawn shop on a corner in Pittsburgh, Pennsylvania," and we claimed that as part of our heritage.

Our environment was entirely different from Lake Wobegon, but I understand the spirit in which Garrison Keillor writes about his mythical hometown, the little town in which "all the women are strong, all the men are good-looking, and all the children are above average."

Sometimes our pride in our hometowns is expressed in slogans. Dallas is The Big D; New York is the Big Apple; Chicago is the Windy City. In the middle of Kansas there is a place called "mid-America."

Israel had its special cities, too, but they were special for very different reasons. To be sure, there was pride in the many hundreds of cities in which the Jews lived. We have seen something of Caleb's special fascination with Hebron, and Joshua was certainly proud of his hill town of Timnath Serah. Everyone would have been proud of the town he had captured as part of the overall Jewish conquest of Palestine. In fact, I detect a note of this in the careful listing of towns allotted to each of the Jewish tribes. They are noted for the record, of course—like title deeds to property. But there must also have been a measure of pride as people looked over the list and saw their own towns. The record was a way of saying that each town was important.

Still, there were cities that were particularly special, as I have suggested. They fell into two classes. First, there were the forty-eight cities of the Levites, the priests. These were scattered throughout the land of the other twelve tribes (Ephraim and Manasseh, who had descended from Joseph, were each a tribe and thus made twelve tribes in addition to the Levites). Second, there were cities of refuge—three on the eastern side of the Jordan River and three on the western side. The cities of refuge are described in Joshua 20. The towns of the Levites are described in chapter 21.

Cities of Refuge

The six cities of refuge were taken from among the forty-eight cities of the Levites. They were established as refuge cities at the specific command of God, which is recorded in Numbers 35 and repeated with some variations in Deuteronomy 19. (There are two briefer mentions of these cities in Exodus 21:12, 13 and Deuteronomy 4:41–43.)

The need for these cities grew out of the fact that in the ancient world, and to some extent in the Near East even today, there was a custom according to which, if a member of a family or clan was killed by someone, either intentionally or accidentally, the family would gather together and appoint one of its members to be an "avenger of blood" for his relative. This was a world in which the basic legal maxim was "an eye for an eye and a tooth for a tooth." So if a member of the family was killed, it became the duty of the avenger of blood to track down and kill the murderer. Clearly, there was a certain primitive justice in this system. But a person could be killed by accident, and if that were the situation, it would be an injustice if the avenger were allowed to proceed.

Moses was instructed to establish cities of refuge into which the *accidental* manslayer, not a true murderer, could flee for safety. For instance, Numbers 35 imagines a situation in which two men are working together chopping wood, when suddenly the head of one man's ax flies off, killing the other man. That is a situation in which an avenger of blood could be appointed to kill the killer. But in this case, the manslayer would be innocent of any real evil. So instead of waiting patiently for his fate, having to flee the country like a fugitive, or going into hiding, he would immediately run for the nearest refuge city before the avenger of blood could overtake him.

Once in the city, the frightened man was to appear before the elders, as the text in Joshua shows. He was to state his case, explaining why the death was accidental. Then, if the elders of the city judged that there was no malice aforethought and the death was indeed accidental, they were to admit him to the city, where he was to live in safety. It was necessary for him to remain there until the death of the high priest serving at that time. After that, he could return home in safety.

It is important to note that this was not an arrangement by which a murderer could avoid justice. The one who murdered another was to be judicially executed. This was a device designed to save someone guilty of manslaughter but innocent of murder.

I have been greatly helped by Francis Schaeffer's treatment of this special institution. He makes the following points in his commentary.

1. Instead of treating life lightly, as the practical outworking of much of our law seems to do, the appointment of *the cities of refuge emphasized the value of man made in God's image.* In other words, the institution of these cities was motivated by the same concern that required death for a murderer. Back in the early pages of Genesis, after the great flood, God told Moses, ". . . From each man . . . I will demand an accounting for the

life of his fellow man. 'Whoever sheds the blood of man, by man shall his blood be shed; for in the image of God has God made man' '' (Genesis 9:5, 6). Capital punishment was established because man is made in God's image and is therefore too valuable to be wantonly destroyed. In Exodus, the principle is: "Anyone who strikes a man and kills him shall surely be put to death" (Exodus 21:12). But by precisely the same principle, no one should be put to death if the death caused by him was accidental. Therefore, Exodus goes on to say, "However, if he does not do it intentionally, but God lets it happen, he is to flee to a place I will designate" (v. 13).

Schaeffer writes, "Because God exists and because he has a character, we live in a true moral universe. Murder breaks the law of the universe. This means that the murderer has true moral guilt before God—something our modern generation knows nothing or little about—and this guilt must be taken seriously."[1]

2. Because the cities of refuge were open to foreigners living in Israel as well as to Jews, as Joshua 20:9 indicates, *we have here a genuinely universal code of justice.* Many societies have had a measure of justice for their own citizens while denying the protection of those laws to outsiders. This was not the case in Israel. In Israel, the foreigner enjoyed the same rights as the Jew. Thus Israel testified to the oneness of the human race and the answerability of each person to the one true God.

3. Since each of these points is based on the religious awareness of the Jewish people that all persons are made by the one God and are made in his image, this law, as well as the other laws of Israel, testified to the fact that *the only proper foundation of any universal law is God's character.*

Schaeffer puts it like this:

---

1. Francis A. Schaeffer, *Joshua and the Flow of Biblical History* (Downers Grove, Ill.: InterVarsity Press, 1975), pp. 194, 195.

The cities of refuge were levitical cities, that is, they had something to do with God. The person taking refuge had to stay in the city until the death of the high priest so he would be reminded that the civil laws were related to God. They did not just exist in a sociological vacuum. Unlike modern man, the people of the Old Testament and of Christian communities after the Reformation did not view civil law as basically sociological. To them it was not founded primarily on a social contract. Civil law was related to society, but not only to society. It was ultimately related to the existence and character of God. This is important. Law which comes from God can provide something fixed. Today's sociological law is relativistic.[2]

It should be evident from these points that the existence of the cities of refuge in Israel has much to say to the legal systems of our modern Western cultures.

"Other Refuge Have I None"

They also say much as an illustration of the value of the work of Christ for sinners, which Schaeffer likewise points out. The illustration is not perfect, of course. For one thing, the cities of refuge were for people who were innocent of real crime. We are not innocent; on the contrary, we are woefully guilty in God's sight. Again, though they were carefully spaced throughout the land, the cities of refuge would nevertheless often be far from the poor fugitive, and it would be only at the end of a desperate race that he might find safety. Christ is always at hand. Still, in spite of these obvious differences, many have noted that Christ is indeed a refuge for us, like the refuge cities of Israel, and that many characteristics of these cities have spiritual parallels.

First, it was the duty of the Jews to clearly indicate the way to the cities of refuge. Deuteronomy 19:3 says that roads were to be built to these cities. Nonbiblical sources tell us that the aid to

2. *Ibid.*, p. 193.

these fugitives was even more extensive. Bridges were built over ravines, so the fugitive could take the shortest route possible. The roads were carefully repaired each spring. At every crossroads, special signs read, "Refuge! Refuge!" No one wanted a fugitive to take the wrong road. Moreover, the signs were made large, so that even a man who was running hard could read them without stopping. This is a good parallel to our responsibility to make the way to Christ easily accessible to the lost. Apart from Christ, the sinner is a dead man. Who will help him find the way to that city? We must build bridges, repair roads, and erect signs leading to Jesus. Moreover, we must stand in the way and point this refuge out. We must shout, "This is the way! There alone is safety!"

Second, the doors of the cities of refuge were always unlocked. That was an important and unusual feature for an ancient town. In those days, towns locked their gates at night to protect those within them from robbers, vandals, or any who would do the residents harm. In times of war, the gates would be always locked; not so the cities of refuge. The gates of these cities were always to be open, just as the arms of Christ are always open to receive any who will come to him. Jesus said, ". . . Whoever comes to me I will never drive away" (John 6:37). The last chapter of the Bible reads, "The Spirit and the bride say, 'Come!' And let him who hears say, 'Come!' Whoever is thirsty, let him come; and whoever wishes, let him take the free gift of the water of life" (Revelation 22:17).

Third, the cities of refuge were not only for Jews but for people of all races. Similarly, the salvation available in Jesus Christ is for all. It does not matter who you are. You may be young or old. You may be a Jew or a Gentile. You may be black or white, rich or poor, male or female, educated or uneducated, advantaged or disadvantaged. It does not matter, for the way of salvation is available. You need only give up whatever illusions of safety you may now have, acknowledge your danger, and flee to Jesus.

Finally, if an ancient manslayer did not flee to one of the cities of refuge, there was no hope for him; there was no other provision in the law of Israel by which he might be saved. If he did not flee there, the avenger of blood would overtake him, and he would be slain. You, too, are pursued by an untiring and inescapable avenger: death. You may live long, but though you outlast even Methuselah, you will eventually be stricken down by this dread enemy. Who knows? You may be stricken this year, this month, even in the very hour you read these words. How are you to escape this enemy? There is only one way: Jesus. You must flee to him. Jesus said, "I am the resurrection and the life. He who believes in me will live, even though he dies; and whoever lives and believes in me will never die . . ." (John 11:25, 26).

The author of Hebrews was probably thinking of the cities of refuge when he wrote of those ". . . who have fled to take hold of the hope offered to [them] . . ." (Hebrews 6:18).

The Priestly Cities

Joshua 21 is the last chapter in the book dealing with the distribution of the people of Israel in the land. It concerns the apportionment of forty-eight special cities to the Levites. These were scattered throughout the land so that the benefit of the Levites' presence, service, and teaching might be widely available.

This was a wonderful thing, because it was an example of God turning what was originally a curse into a blessing. Back in Genesis 49, Jacob had a particularly harsh word for Simeon and Levi, his second and third sons. He said, ". . . I will scatter them in Jacob and disperse them in Israel" (v. 7). This was because years before these two brothers had led in the massacre of the Shechemites, which Jacob said made him ". . . a stench to the Canaanites . . ." (Genesis 34:30). The scattering of the descendants of these two brothers through the land was their punishment, a way of saying that they were to receive no inheritance.

In Simeon's case, this was fulfilled by having his descendants live in Judah's territory, as we saw in chapter twelve. It was a punishment, but it was a punishment mixed with blessing, since Judah remained close to the things of God throughout its long history and Simeon inevitably benefited from Judah's faithfulness. For example, although the northern kingdom of Israel, containing ten of the twelve tribes, fell to the Assyrians in 721 B.C., Judah (which contained Simeon) endured until 587 B.C.— more than one hundred additional years. So Simeon was even blessed in his judgment.

The case is even more striking with Levi, which is our chief concern here. Levi was scattered throughout Israel in the forty-eight Levitical cities. In addition, the Levites traveled back and forth to perform their share of the duties connected with temple worship. So although the descendants of Levi had no land of their own, it was nevertheless no small honor for them to have been made priests. It was said of them that they had ''no portion'' in the land because ''their portion was the LORD'' himself.

Moreover, they produced great leaders among the people. With the exception of the tribe of Judah, which produced most of the kings, the tribe of Levi contributed more distinguished leaders to Israel than any other.

Moses was a Levite. Moses was born in Egypt during the greatest oppression of the Jewish people. He had godly parents, Amram and Jochebed, both of whom were of the Levitical tribe. He was more highly educated than anyone else of his day. He held a position of great privilege and power in Egypt. It is possible that he could have become a future pharaoh. But Moses did not side with the Egyptians. He sided with his own people. Hebrews tells us:

> By faith Moses, when he had grown up, refused to be known as the son of Pharaoh's daughter. He chose to be mistreated along with the people of God rather than to enjoy the pleasures of sin for a short time. He regarded disgrace for the sake of Christ as of greater value than the treasures of Egypt, because he was looking ahead to his reward. By faith he left Egypt, not

fearing the king's anger; he persevered because he saw him who is invisible. By faith he kept the Passover and the sprinkling of blood, so that the destroyer of the firstborn would not touch the firstborn of Israel.

Hebrews 11:24–28

Aaron was a Levite. He was Moses' brother and was given special duties as the high priest of Israel. The first book of Chronicles says, ". . . Aaron was set apart, he and his descendants forever, to consecrate the most holy things, to offer sacrifices before the LORD, to minister before him and to pronounce blessings in his name forever" (1 Chronicles 23:13).

Phinehas was a special leader in the tribe of Levi. He was the third high priest, and he served faithfully in that role for nineteen years. He is chiefly known for an incident recorded in Numbers 25. The people had fallen into sexual immorality with the women of Moab, who had invited them to the sacrifices to their gods. As a result, the judgment of God in the form of a plague had fallen on the people. Phinehas was offended by this wickedness. So when he saw Zimri, a member of the tribe of Simeon, take a Moabite woman into his tent, he snatched up a spear, followed them, and drove the spear through Zimri into the woman's body. Because of this, the plague was stopped and God praised Phinehas for his zeal. God said, "I am making my covenant of peace with him. He and his descendants will have a covenant of a lasting priesthood, because he was zealous for the honor of his God and made atonement for the Israelites" (Numbers 25:12, 13).

Eli was a Levite. Eli lived to be ninety-eight years old and was a priest in Shiloh. He served as a judge in Israel for forty years (1 Samuel 4:12–18).

Ezra was a Levite. Ezra was a distinguished scribe who served with Nehemiah at the time of the return of the people of Israel from Babylon. He wrote the book of Ezra, the first of the postcaptivity writings.

John the Baptist was a Levite. He was the son of Zacharias, who was a priest in the division of Abijah, and Elizabeth, who was in the line of descent from Aaron (Luke 1:5). God called John to be a forerunner of Jesus Christ in fulfillment of the last words of the Old Testament: "See, I will send you the prophet Elijah before that great and dreadful day of the LORD comes. He will turn the hearts of the fathers to their children, and the hearts of the children to their fathers . . ." (Malachi 4:5, 6). Jesus praised John extravagantly, saying, "I tell you the truth: Among those born of women there has not risen anyone greater than John the Baptist . . ." (Matthew 11:11).

What an encouragement this should be to us! In the scattering of Levi we see God's righteous judgment on sin. But we also see judgment turned to blessing. If you are suffering from what others have done—perhaps from the sin of a parent, as the descendants of Simeon and Levi suffered for the sin of their parents—do not think you are excluded from God's favor or that it is impossible for you to gain God's favor again by godly living. God punishes children for the sin of the fathers ". . . to the third and fourth generation of those who hate [him]" (Exodus 20:5), but he also "repents" of evil and brings blessing where he sees repentance (Exodus 32:14; Jeremiah 18:8; 26:3, 13; Joel 2:13).

Do not despair even if you are suffering for your own sins. I have on my desk a card containing a spiritual quotation from Washington Irving, the American writer. Irving said, "It lightens the stroke to draw near to him who handles the rod." That is true. If you are suffering from sin, draw near to God and find that he is far more ready to transmute the punishment than you are to come to him.[3]

---

3. The study of Levi is adapted from a longer study in James Montgomery Boice, *Genesis,* vol. 3 (Grand Rapids: Zondervan Publishing House, 1987), pp. 274–279.

Chapter Fifteen

Farewell to Arms
Joshua 22:1–34

> *Then Joshua summoned the Reubenites, the Gadites and the half-tribe of Manasseh and said to them, "You have done all that Moses the servant of the LORD commanded, and you have obeyed me in everything I commanded. For a long time now—to this very day— you have not deserted your brothers but have carried out the mission the LORD your God gave you. Now that the LORD your God has given your brothers rest as he promised, return to your homes in the land that Moses the servant of the LORD gave you on the other side of the Jordan. But be very careful to keep the commandment and the law that Moses the servant of the LORD gave you: to love the LORD your God, to walk in all his ways, to obey his commands, to hold fast to him and to serve him with all your heart and all your soul."*
>
> Joshua 22:1–5

Most commentaries on Joshua trail off after dealing with the partition of Canaan among the twelve tribes. This is understandable, I suppose, since it is difficult to deal with Joshua 13–21 at great length, and after commentators scurry through them, the momentum of that study whisks them to the end in at best one or two more chapters.

But study of Joshua suffers from such precipitous endings, and one of the things that suffers is chapter 22, in which Joshua dismisses the two and a half tribes that had been promised land east of the Jordan River. This is unfortunate for several reasons. The chapter contains important instructions for these people, instructions just as important in their own way as Joshua's farewell instructions to the leaders of Israel in chapter 23 and his farewell sermon to the people of Israel as a whole in chapter 24. Again, the chapter contains a moving farewell, and that leads into what is certainly one of the most instructive incidents in all the long years of the campaign.

Winning the Peace

The theme of each of these last chapters of Joshua is the need to acknowledge and serve God in peace as well as in war. The setting is the time of transition. For seven long years the people had followed Joshua in an aggressive and far-ranging conquest of the Promised Land. They had been faithful to God all that time. True, there had been a few lapses. Achan had disobeyed God by taking some of the spoil of Jericho, which he had been forbidden to do. Joshua had neglected to seek the mind of God in the initial attack on Ai. Later he and the people had been deceived by the wiles of the Gibeonites. But those were not great lapses, and they had been early in the campaign. As far as we can tell, the seven years of fighting had been marked mostly by Israel's faithfulness to God and the task before them.

But what of the peace? Nations often lose in peace what they have gained in war. Would Israel abandon its high level of spiritual commitment and integrity and gradually fall into disobedience and paganism? Or would the people remain faithful to God? Those questions were on Joshua's mind and heart as he challenged first the eastern tribes, then the leaders, and eventually the entire company of the people.

When Joshua spoke to the Reubenites, Gadites, and half-tribe of Manasseh, who were about to return to their homes on the eastern side of the Jordan, he stressed three things: their past obedience to his commands and the commands of Moses; the faithfulness of God in giving them the land he had promised and bringing them the peace they were currently enjoying; and their obligation to continue to keep God's commandments. In amplifying this last point, Joshua said, "But be very careful to keep the commandment and the law that Moses the servant of the LORD gave you: to love the LORD your God, to walk in all his ways, to obey his commands, to hold fast to him and to serve him with all your heart and all your soul" (Joshua 22:5).

It is not difficult to see that this is precisely what we are to do in our time. Indeed, that last phrase, drawn from Deuteronomy 6:5, reminds us of the Lord's identification of this verse as the first and great commandment: "Love the Lord your God with all your heart and with all your soul and with all your mind" (Matthew 22:37). Fulfilling that commandment means walking in God's ways, holding fast to him, and serving him wholeheartedly, as Joshua explained.

An Emotional Parting

I am certain that Francis Schaeffer is right when he asks us to use our imagination at this point and try to feel the tremendous emotion involved in the parting of these comrades in arms.[1] The text does not speak of these emotions. But we must remember that these men had fought side by side in a conquest that lasted longer than either of our world wars. A special bond would have developed among them in such circumstances. Even today we read in the paper of certain emotional gatherings of veterans, perhaps those who fought in a particular campaign of the

1. Francis A. Schaeffer, *Joshua and the Flow of Biblical History* (Downers Grove, Ill.: InterVarsity Press, 1975), p. 174.

European war or who stormed one of the Pacific islands as part of the war against Japan. It would have been like that for these veterans of the Jewish campaigns. As the time came for them to part, soldiers would have passed through the camp saying good-bye to their comrades. Here was a brother who had saved another's life as they had pursued the soldiers of the southern coalition at Gibeon. Here was one who helped storm the fortified walls of Hebron. As I say, it must have been an emotional and very moving moment.

But at last the parting took place, and the two and a half tribes of Reuben, Gad, and Manasseh moved east and eventually made their way to the Jordan. For their own part, the western tribes prepared to disperse to their own territories.

Suddenly word came that something unexpected and terrible was happening. The eastern tribes were building an altar. The text says, "When they came to Geliloth near the Jordan in the land of Canaan, the Reubenites, the Gadites and the half-tribe of Manasseh built an imposing altar there by the Jordan" (Joshua 22:10). This was no light matter. An altar other than the altar at Shiloh, where the tabernacle of the Lord stood, symbolized a break with worship of the true God. It meant apostasy. The text then says, "When the Israelites heard that they had built the altar on the border of Canaan at Geliloth near the Jordan on the Israelite side, the whole assembly of Israel gathered at Shiloh to go to war against them" (vv. 11, 12).

Think of it! These men had just parted under the most moving circumstances. They were sick of war and were rejoicing in the long-awaited peace. But suddenly, as soon as they heard that the two and a half tribes of Reuben, Gad, and Manasseh were constructing a rival altar, they snatched up their arms again and prepared to march against them.

Schaeffer says, "That is just terrific!" These men were not warmongers. On the contrary, they were tired of fighting. They were not angry or jealous or resentful of their brothers across the river. They were comrades. Why then were the western tribes prepared to go to war against the eastern tribes? There is only one explanation. Although they loved their brothers to the east and were certainly tired of fighting, they nevertheless loved the honor of God more and were determined to let nothing intrude on that honor. They were zealous for God. Schaeffer says, "I would to God that the church of the twentieth century would learn this lesson. The holiness of the God who exists demands that there be no compromise in the area of truth. Tears? I am sure there were tears, but there had to be battle if there was rebellion against God."[2]

Love and Holiness

But the war did not start immediately, and in this there is another great lesson. The western tribes were ready to go to war, but before they marched against the eastern tribes, they dispatched a delegation to investigate the situation and see if the error they believed to be unfolding could not be straightened out. This was a demonstration of both love and concern for God's holiness. Note these elements.

The delegation from the west was forthright in describing what concerned them. Today we are often so reluctant to alienate anybody or give anyone offense that we tone down our concerns, suggest that they might not really be so important, after all, or forget them entirely. Not so this Jewish delegation. The delegation was composed of ten men, one leader from each of the ten western tribes, all under the oversight of Phinehas, son of Eleazar the priest. These went to the two and a half eastern tribes and said:

> The whole assembly of the LORD says: "How could you break faith with the God of Israel like this? How could you turn away from the LORD and build yourselves an altar in rebellion against him now? Was not the sin of Peor enough for us? Up to this very day we have not cleansed ourselves from

2. Ibid., p. 175.

that sin, even though a plague fell on the community of the
LORD! And are you now turning away from the LORD? If you
rebel against the LORD today, tomorrow he will be angry with
the whole community of Israel.''

Joshua 22:16–18

These are clear words. Apostasy is called apostasy. Moreover,
a clear connection is made between the disobedience of one and
the sufferings of many. Morality is not individualistic. Therefore,
if those who claim to be God's people do not live for him
faithfully and obediently, others who are trying to follow the
Lord will suffer.

Do we believe that? If we do, can we be as tolerant of apostasy
and loose living by those who claim to be Christians as we
apparently are? Would it not be the case, if we really believed
these things, that we would be zealous for God's honor?

**The peoples of the west were willing to pay any price to
reclaim their lost brothers.** It is important to see this. The
western tribes did not merely demonstrate their love for those
they thought were erring by going to talk with them before
attacking them, though that was significant in itself and is
something from which we should learn. They did something even
greater. They offered their own lands if that could be the means
of drawing the eastern peoples back to faithful worship of
Jehovah. Note what they said: ''If the land you possess is defiled,
come over to the LORD's land, where the LORD's tabernacle stands,
and share the land with us . . .'' (v. 19). In other words, ''If the
cause of your apostasy is the traditions of the land in which you
live, don't live there. Come over to where we live, and we will
give you some of our cities, some of our land. Only do not rebel
against the Lord.''

This is costly love. But this is the kind of love that wins people
to God. Often, when we do actually practice discipline (and
discipline is sometimes necessary, particularly in our spiritually

lax age), we do it in a self-righteous or self-serving way that exalts ourselves and usually repels the other party. How much different and how much more effective it would be if we paid a personal price in our attempts to reclaim those who are erring.

When the concerns of the western people were explained, the two and a half eastern tribes agreed with the charges. This is important, too, because it shows that these were true believers in God and not imposters. Not a word in their reply indicates that the peoples of the east thought lightly of erecting false altars. They did not say, as many do in our day when the commands of God are proclaimed, "But that's just your opinion." That response is a strong indication that the person making it is not saved, for no one who is possessed by the Spirit of God can be cavalier with God's commandments.

The words "but that's just your opinion" are an evasion, you see. It is true that anything any of us honestly expresses is our opinion, but that is not the point. The point is, is that opinion right? Is that the standard? Is that what God has spoken? If there is doubt at this point, believers may stop and work through it together to see if that is what God has indeed said or if there has been misunderstanding or distortion. That examination should go on in the church all the time. But the one thing the true believer cannot do is dismiss the charge as if such things were relative. If God has spoken, we must agree with his words and conform our lives to them—if we are truly his disciples.

Notice, too, that the tribes of Reuben, Gad, and the half tribe of Manasseh did not only agree with the nature of the charges but also agreed with the rightness of judgment—if the charges were true. ". . . If this has been in rebellion or disobedience to the LORD, do not spare us this day. If we have built our own altar to turn away from the LORD and to offer burnt offerings and grain offerings, or to sacrifice fellowship offerings on it, may the LORD himself call us to account" (Joshua 22:22, 23). In admitting the

rightness of judgment, they also admitted the rightness of the
standard their friends were upholding.

A Happy Ending

Often a confrontation like this in the church ends badly—to our
shame. But in this case all ended well. The tribes who were
crossing the Jordan explained that they had not built their altar to
establish schismatic worship of another god but rather as a
reminder of the history they shared with the western tribes
because of their continuing worship and service of Jehovah.

They explained their actions this way:

> We did it for fear that some day your descendants might say
> to ours, "What do you have to do with the LORD, the God of
> Israel? The LORD has made the Jordan a boundary between us
> and you—you Reubenites and Gadites! You have no share in
> the LORD." So your descendants might cause ours to stop
> fearing the LORD. That is why we said, "Let us get ready and
> build an altar—but not for burnt offerings or sacrifices." On
> the contrary, it is to be a witness between us and you and the
> generations that follow, that we will worship the LORD at his
> sanctuary with our burnt offerings, sacrifices and fellowship
> offerings. Then in the future your descendants will not be able
> to say to ours, "You have no share in the LORD." . . . Far be
> it from us to rebel against the LORD and turn away from him
> today by building an altar for burnt offerings, grain offerings
> and sacrifices, other than the altar of the LORD our God that
> stands before his tabernacle.
>
> Joshua 22:24–27, 29

In other words, the altar by the Jordan was not to be a functional
altar but a memorial or reminder of the altar at Shiloh, and it was
not to mark a division but a union among the twelve tribes.

Why did this story turn out well when there was so much room
for disagreement? It was because of the two steps already
mentioned. Schaeffer says:

First, there was a clear agreement on the importance of doctrine and truth, an understanding that the holiness of God demands bowing before him and obeying his commands. Remember Joshua's words as he sent the people away to the other side of the Jordan: "Take diligent heed . . . to love the LORD your God, and to walk in all his ways, and to keep his commandments." There was a happy ending because the people did this.

Second, those who were courageous in standing for truth were also courageous in acting in love. If there had only been a stand for truth, there would never have been a happy ending. There would have only been war because the ten tribes would have torn across the river and killed the other Israelites without talking to anybody. There would have been sadness in the midst of misunderstanding. But because of the love of God, the tribes talked to each other openly, and the love and holiness of God were able to come together. Psalm 85 speaks of the righteousness of God and the love of God kissing each other (v. 10). This is what happened.[3]

In the final analysis, the Christian has only one basic duty in life, and that is to show forth the reality of the existence of God and his character in the midst of a rebellious world. This is not always easy to do, not even among Christians. But it is something God blesses if we seriously apply ourselves to that calling. The world knows nothing like this. In place of holiness and truth, it has relativism. It has truth for you and truth for me, one standard of morality for you and another for someone else. But instead of everyone getting along wonderfully, as that kind of relativism would seem to guarantee, the world is filled with misunderstanding, selfishness, and cruel hatred.

As Christians we have a chance to show that a combined zeal for truth and love lays the basis for harmony and in the final analysis is the only thing really blessed by God.

3. Ibid., pp. 180, 181.

Chapter Sixteen

Passing the Torch
Joshua 23:1–16

*After a long time had passed and the L*ORD *had given Israel rest from all their enemies around them, Joshua, by then old and well advanced in years, summoned all Israel—their elders, leaders, judges and officials—and said to them: "I am old and well advanced in years. You yourselves have seen everything the L*ORD *your God has done to all these nations for your sake; it was the L*ORD *your God who fought for you. Remember how I have allotted as an inheritance for your tribes all the land of the nations that remain—the nations I conquered— between the Jordan and the Great Sea in the west. The L*ORD *your God himself will drive them out of your way. He will push them out before you. . . .*

*"Be very strong; be careful to obey all that is written in the Book of the Law of Moses, without turning aside to the right or to the left. Do not associate with these nations that remain among you; do not invoke the names of their gods or swear by them. You must not serve them or bow down to them. But you are to hold fast to the L*ORD *your God, as you have until now."*

Joshua 23:1–8

There is something poignant and stirring about the last words of great men, particularly if they are a charge to their successors.

In American history we think of Washington's farewell to the Continental Army or of Douglas MacArthur's address to Congress: "An old soldier who tried to do his duty as God gave him the light to see that duty. Good-bye."

We turn to the Bible particularly for these moving charges. In the last verses of Genesis, Joseph, the central figure of the last third of that book, is dying and has gathered his brothers about him. He wants to remind them of God's past blessing and of his promised future intervention on their behalf. He says, "I am about to die. But God will surely come to your aid and take you up out of this land to the land he promised on oath to Abraham, Isaac and Jacob. . . . God will surely come to your aid, and then you must carry my bones up from this place" (Genesis 50:24, 25).

Again, we think of Moses' farewell, recorded in the last chapters of Deuteronomy. They contain the so-called "Song of Moses" and Moses' final blessing on the tribes.

The New Testament contains Paul's farewell to the Ephesian elders at a stopover on his final trip to Jerusalem:

> I know that none of you among whom I have gone about preaching the kingdom will ever see me again. Therefore, I declare to you today that I am innocent of the blood of all men. For I have not hesitated to proclaim to you the whole will of God. Guard yourselves and all the flock of which the Holy Spirit has made you overseers. Be shepherds of the church of God, which he bought with his own blood. I know that after I leave, savage wolves will come in among you and will not spare the flock. . . . So be on your guard! Remember that for three years I never stopped warning each of you night and day with tears.
>
> Acts 20:25–29, 31

The ending of Joshua is like this. A long period of time had passed since the events of the previous chapter. At the end of the conquest, Joshua was probably about ninety years of age (forty years in Egypt, according to Josephus; forty years in the wilderness; and seven years in the conquest), and at the time of his death, recorded in Joshua 24:29, he was one hundred and ten. So there is a twenty- or twenty-three-year interval between Joshua 22 and 23, and Joshua, knowing that he was soon to pass from the scene, wanted to give a final charge to his successors.

Actually, he gave two of them. The last chapter of the book contains a charge to the people as a whole assembled at Shechem. The twenty-third chapter, which we are to study now, contains a charge to the nation's chief men: Israel's "elders, leaders, judges and officials." Caleb would be there, and Phinehas, the son of Eleazar the priest. So would the soldiers who had fought with Joshua through the various campaigns. Most of these men would have been mere youths back then. Now they would be grown. They would have families. All would have risen to positions of important leadership in the nation.

What was Joshua to say on such an occasion? What would he emphasize to these new leaders as he passed the torch to them?

What God Had Done

In this chapter Joshua mentions a number of very important things, and the first of them, quite naturally, is a reminder of what God had previously done for the people. Joshua's reminder has three parts: the military victories, the partitioning of the land at God's direction, and the completion of the settlement, some of which was still future but which Joshua regarded as certain. His words are: "... 'I am old and well advanced in years. You yourselves have seen everything the Lord your God has done to all these nations for your sake; it was the Lord your God who fought for you. Remember how I have allotted as an inheritance for your tribes all the land of the nations that remain—the nations I conquered—between the Jordan and the Great Sea in the west. The Lord your God himself will drive them out of your way. He will push them out before you, and you will take possession of their land, as the LORD your God promised you' " (Joshua 23:2–5).

I said that Joshua "naturally" reminded the people of these things. But although that is true in one sense—it is natural that Joshua should have spoken of the Lord's past acts on Israel's behalf—it is also unnatural in that we do not naturally think this way ourselves. On the contrary, we separate ourselves from God's actions.

We separate ourselves from what God has done by making faith a matter of subjective feelings, as if what matters is how we feel about religion rather than knowing and acting on what God has done. We do not generally admit this, of course, and we believe that God *has* done great acts of redemption for us in the past. But often this becomes less important to us than how we feel now, and we begin to act on our feelings rather than upon what we know of God and God's ways. Joshua did not want the people of Israel to do that. In time they would be attracted to the world and its ways, to the religious practices and morals of the surrounding pagan cultures. At that time, these ways would seem "good" to Israel, and the pleasures of sin would "feel" desirable. They were not to defect from a proper worship of God for that reason, because they knew certain things about God: He had acted for them powerfully in their deliverance from Egypt and in the conquest and had thereby shown himself to be the true God.

The people were to ground their feelings on this knowledge, rather than the other way around.

Second, we separate ourselves from God's acts in history by thinking of faith as a "leap" over evidence. The Danish philosopher and churchman Søren Kierkegaard was the fountain of this way of thinking, having spoken of the "leap of faith," and many churchmen have picked it up since, thinking that somehow it saves us from the embarrassment of sound

Christian apologetics. It does nothing of the sort. It is true that the
"leap of faith" abandons apologetics, but it also launches
Christianity upon a boundless sea where many have been
shipwrecked. The Bible knows nothing of this "leap of faith." It
says, "Look at what God has done for you in history. Remember
his acts. Reason about these things, and build upon them." The
Bible does not abandon evidence. It builds faith on reason, and
understanding on faith.

Our Present Obligations

The second theme in Joshua's charge to the leaders of Israel as he
passed the torch of leadership to them was their present obliga-
tions. It was not enough to know that God had acted for them in
the past. It was also necessary for them to order their lives in
certain ways because of that action. There are two requirements.

Obedience.   Obedience is a natural emphasis for a soldier such
as Joshua to make, particularly since it had been the charge given
to him by God at the very start of the campaigns. But it was more
than that. It is a duty incumbent upon all God's people. The
words Joshua uses in this charge are an important echo of what he
had been told to do earlier, and are a deliberate reference to them.
At the beginning, God had appeared to Joshua to assure him that
he would be with him as he had been with Moses. Joshua was to
be careful to obey all that Moses had spoken. God said, "Be
strong and courageous, because you will lead these people to
inherit the land I swore to their forefathers to give them. Be
strong and very courageous. Be careful to obey all the law my
servant Moses gave you; do not turn from it to the right or to the
left, that you may be successful wherever you go. Do not let this
Book of the Law depart from your mouth; meditate on it day and
night, so that you may be careful to do everything written in it.
Then you will be prosperous and successful" (Joshua 1:6–8).

Joshua had done this. He had obeyed God, fulfilling the law of Moses exactly. Now he wished to pass on a similar charge to God's people.

Joshua said, "Be very strong; be careful to obey all that is written in the Book of the Law of Moses, without turning aside to the right or to the left. Do not associate with these nations that remain among you; do not invoke the names of their gods or swear by them. You must not serve them or bow down to them. But you are to hold fast to the LORD your God, as you have until now" (Joshua 23:6–8).

Two things should be noted. First, there is a connection between the demand to obey God's commands and the previously stated fact that God had done great things on the people's behalf. This is the same connection we find at the start of the Ten Commandments. It is because God had brought the people out of Egypt, out of the land of slavery, that they were to have no other gods before him. There is a connection between God's having given Israel the land and the obedience required.

Second, there is a continuing appeal to the written law of God given through Moses. This is a most important standard. It is not merely that the people of Israel were urged to live upright, moral, consistent, and productive lives. That is what people try to do today, apart from God's written standard in Scripture, but it does not work. Joshua did not give some vague appeal to an undefined moral code. He presented them with Scripture, ". . . with all that is written in the Book of the Law of Moses . . ." (v. 6), and they were promised God's favor and blessing if they continued to live by that standard. It is the same today. In fact, it is the same standard. That standard has been amplified over the centuries during which the Bible was written. In the very next chapter we find that "Joshua recorded these things in the Book of the Law of God . . ." (Joshua 24:26). In other words, at this point, the Book of Joshua was added to the canon as an authoritative revelation from God for his people. But the standard is the same in all these books and is our standard today. In this respect, Joshua's charge is contemporary.

Love for God.   It is not only obedience to God's law that is urged on the people. That has been a concern all along. Here, in addition to the demand to obey God in all things, there is the added obligation to love the God who had blessed them so abundantly. Joshua says, "So be very careful to love the LORD your God" (Joshua 23:11). What did Joshua mean by loving God? We have the answer in the way he referred to love in the previous chapter, when giving his charge to the two and a half tribes that were departing to their lands on the far side of the Jordan River. There he had said, "Be very careful to keep the commandment and the law that Moses the servant of the LORD gave you: to love the LORD your God, to walk in all his ways, to obey his commands, to hold fast to him and to serve him with all your heart and all your soul" (Joshua 22:5). That is a reference to Deuteronomy 6:5, the verse Jesus called the greatest of all the commandments. It is a definition of what love for God means. Love means *walking* in God's ways, *obeying* God's commands, *holding fast* to God, and *serving* God with all one's heart and soul.

Obeying God (the first point) and loving God (the second point) go together. Do not say you love God if you are not obeying his commands in the Bible. To claim that is hypocrisy. If you love God, you *will* keep his commands. And it goes with that principle that if you attempt to obey those commands and sincerely walk in God's ways, you will find yourself coming to love God more and more.

Focus on the Family

The third section of Joshua's charge deals with a brand-new problem: the intermarrying of Jews with the people of the land.

Joshua says, "But if you turn away and ally youselves with the survivors of these nations that remain among you and if you intermarry with them and associate with them, then you may be sure that the LORD your God will no longer drive out these nations before you. Instead, they will become snares and traps for you, whips on your backs and thorns in your eyes, until you perish from this good land, which the LORD your God has given you" (Joshua 23:12, 13).

The intermarrying of Jews with other peoples had not been much of a problem up to now. But Joshua was a keen observer of human nature, and he therefore wisely anticipated the enormous problems Israel would have in this area. The problem was not the problem of racial or ethnic intermarriage, of course, any more than such things are forbidden today. A mixed race had come up out of Egypt, and Moses had himself married a Cushite, that is, an Ethiopian. Rahab was incorporated into Israel. No, the problem was rather what we would call the marrying of a believer with an unbeliever. The people of the land were idolatrous and exceedingly corrupt. That is why God had ordered Israel to destroy them. Joshua foresaw that Jews might marry survivors of these corrupt Canaanite nations and so be drawn away to worship their false gods and practice their degeneracies.

And it happened! This is the sad history of Israel from this period onward. All through the period of the judges and into the time of the kings, Israel fell away from God through just this path. Even after the Babylonian captivity and dispersion, in the time of Ezra and Nehemiah, this is a chief concern. Nehemiah in particular ends on this note.

Do we see the devil's hand in this temptation? I am sure we do. For just as dictators inevitably try to weaken family ties, knowing that if they destroy families they make the winning of people's total allegiance to the state much easier, so the devil knows that if he can destroy the family, he can destroy any effective influence of believers on this world.

Joshua's warnings were not only for Israel. They are warnings for us, also. They are echoed by Paul's well-known admonition: "Do not be yoked together with unbelievers. For what do righteousness and wickedness have in common? Or what fellowship can light have with darkness? What harmony is there between Christ and Belial? . . ." (2 Corinthians 6:14, 15).

Time to Choose

The last point of Joshua's charge to Israel's new leaders was the need to choose; that is, to make a decision to obey and serve God and not to allow oneself to drift along into eventual disobedience. The challenge to choose is not as pointed here as it becomes in chapter 24, but this is the idea, nonetheless.

> Now I am about to go the way of all the earth. You know with all your heart and soul that not one of all the good promises the LORD your God gave you has failed. Every promise has been fulfilled; not one has failed. But just as every good promise of the LORD your God has come true, so the LORD will bring on you all the evil he has threatened, until he has destroyed you from this good land he has given you. If you violate the covenant of the LORD your God, which he commanded you, and go and serve other gods and bow down to them, the LORD's anger will burn against you, and you will quickly perish from the good land he has given you.
>
> Joshua 23:14–16

This is the theme of the book of Deuteronomy and of the ceremony enacted by Joshua on Mount Ebal and Mount Gerizim in obedience to Moses' earlier command. If the people obey, there will be blessing. If they disobey, there will be judgment. They must choose. As far as these conditional promises are concerned, their response alone will make the difference.

But there are inducements, for God never presents a choice as if both sides of the alternative are equal. What strikes me in these last words of Joshua to the elders, leaders, judges, and officials is his fourfold repetition of the word *good*. Twice Joshua speaks of the "good promises the LORD your God gave you" (vv. 14, 15), and twice he speaks of the "good land he has given" (vv. 15, 16).

That is the point, you see. We are to follow and obey God not merely because he is the true God and we should follow him, though that is obvious. It is not even because God's way is the best way, though that is also important. The best of a number of options is not in itself necessarily a "good" way. No, we are urged to follow God because God really is good and because his way really is a good way.

Psalms 34:8 says, "Taste and see that the LORD is *good*; blessed is the man who takes refuge in him."

Psalms 100:5 declares, "The LORD is *good* and his love endures forever."

In Psalms 103:5 David affirms, "He satisfies your desires with *good* things. . . ."

Psalms 69:16 speaks of the *goodness* of God's love.

Psalms 119:39 asserts that all God's "laws are *good*."

Nahum 1:7 observes, "The LORD is *good*, a refuge in times of trouble."

Romans 7:12 argues, "So then, the law is holy, and the commandment is holy, righteous and *good*."

Romans 8:28 says that "in all things God works for the *good* of those who love him, who have been called according to his purpose."

Romans 12:2 admonishes us ". . . to test and approve what God's will is—his *good*, pleasing and perfect will."

James 1:17 declares, "Every *good* and perfect gift is from above, coming down from the Father of the heavenly lights, who does not change like shifting shadows."

In John 10:11, Jesus calls Himself "the *good* shepherd."

Psalms 84:11 affirms, "The LORD God is a sun and shield; the LORD bestows favor and honor; no *good* thing does he withhold from those whose walk is blameless."

These verses are not misrepresentations. God does not lie, and God is master of the understatement. In God's mouth "good" means superlative, tremendous. And isn't this so? Isn't God good? Isn't his way the best of all possible choices? If you agree that it is and that God is indeed good, then you should follow him wholeheartedly. Say, as Joshua himself does in the very next chapter, ". . . As for me and my household, we will serve the LORD" (Joshua 24:15).

Chapter Seventeen

The Captain's Last Sermon
Joshua 24:1–33

"Now fear the Lord and serve him with all faithfulness. Throw away the gods your forefathers worshiped beyond the River and in Egypt, and serve the Lord. But if serving the Lord seems undesirable to you, then choose for yourselves this day whom you will serve, whether the gods your forefathers served beyond the River, or the gods of the Amorites, in whose land you are living. But as for me and my household, we will serve the Lord."

Then the people answered, "Far be it from us to forsake the Lord to serve other gods! It was the Lord our God himself who brought us and our forefathers up out of Egypt, from that land of slavery, and performed those great signs before our eyes. He protected us on our entire journey and among all the nations through which we traveled. And the Lord drove out before us all the nations, including the Amorites, who lived in the land. We too will serve the Lord, because he is our God."

Joshua said to the people, "You are not able to serve the Lord. He is a holy God; he is a jealous God. He will not forgive your rebellion and your sins. If you forsake the Lord and serve foreign gods, he will turn and bring disaster on you and make an end of you, after he has been good to you."

*But the people said to Joshua, "No! We will serve the
LORD."*

*Then Joshua said, "You are witnesses against your-
selves that you have chosen to serve the LORD."*

"Yes, we are witnesses," they replied.

*"Now then," said Joshua, "throw away the foreign
gods that are among you and yield your hearts to the
LORD, the God of Israel."*

*And the people said to Joshua, "We will serve the
LORD our God and obey him."*

Joshua 24:14–24

A number of years ago, when the Committee on Biblical
Exposition was being organized, the founders met to try to define
expository preaching. It was not an easy thing to do. Exposition
involves communicating what a particular portion of Scripture is
all about, but it also involves the application of those truths to us
today and the attempt to move one's hearers to obey those
teachings. At last the committee defined biblical exposition as
"communicating the meaning of a text or passage of Scripture in
terms of contemporary culture, with the specific goal of helping
people to understand and obey the truth of God."

Joshua would have understood and readily concurred in that
definition. He was not called to be a preacher; he was a soldier
and administrator. But as he drew near the end of his life and
looked ahead to the temptations that he knew would come to
Israel to depart from the worship of the true God after his
departure, he turned to preaching in an attempt to keep them as
faithful to God as possible.

We have three sermons of Joshua in the closing three chapters
of this book, each longer than the one before it. The first is in
chapter 22. It was delivered to the two and a half tribes of
Reuben, Gad, and Manasseh which were returning home to their
lands beyond the Jordan River. The second is in chapter 23. It

was spoken to the leaders of Israel: the elders, leaders, judges, and official. The third was spoken to the entire company of the people at a great convocation at Shechem. This occurs in chapter 24. It is a significant feature of these sermons that although they were spoken to different groups of people and contain somewhat different material, they all have essentially the same point: the need of the people to be faithful to and fervently obey God. Joshua was no abstract, unconcerned homilist. He preached for decisions. He was earnest. He preached, as one of the great Puritan preachers once described himself, "as a dying man to dying men."

Joshua's chief burden is in verses 14 and 15. "Now fear the LORD and serve him with all faithfulness. Throw away the gods your forefathers worshiped beyond the River and in Egypt, and serve the LORD. But if serving the LORD seems undesirable to you, then choose for yourselves this day whom you will serve, whether the gods your forefathers served beyond the River, or the gods of the Amorites, in whose land you are living. But as for me and my household, we will serve the LORD."

God of Our Fathers

But Joshua did not begin his sermon at this point. He began by reminding the people of their past and of what God had done for them in bringing them out of the culture of ancient Babylon and then later out of Egypt into the land he had promised to Abraham at the beginning of their history.

The emphasis, of course, is on what God did for them and of the fact that he had done it. There would have been a temptation at the end of these long years of conquest for the people, particularly the soldiers, to think back over their victories and boast of them as their achievements. They might have boasted of their victory at Jericho, Ai, or any one of the many other hundreds of engagements. But Joshua does not allow the people the sin of such reflections. Indeed, he does not say that God did something by using the third person to refer to him. He quotes God, using the first person for God repeatedly and effectively throughout this section:

> *I* took your father Abraham from the land beyond the River. . . . *I* gave him Isaac, and to Isaac *I* gave Jacob and Esau. *I* assigned the hill country of Seir to Esau. . . . *I* sent Moses and Aaron. . . . *I* afflicted the Egyptians by what *I* did there, and *I* brought you out. . . . *I* brought your fathers out of Egypt. . . . *I* brought you to the land of the Amorites. . . . *I* gave them into your hands. *I* destroyed them from before you. . . . When Balak son of Zippor, the king of Moab, prepared to fight against Israel. . . . *I* delivered you out of his hand. . . . The citizens of Jericho fought against you . . . but *I* gave them into your hands. *I* sent the hornet ahead of you. . . . You did not do it with your own sword and bow. So *I* gave you a land on which you did not toil and cities you did not build; and you live in them and eat from vineyards and olive groves that you did not plant.
>
> Joshua 24:3–13, emphasis mine

It would be difficult to stress the sovereign acts of God on his people's behalf more effectively at any length than these verses stress it.

I think of Rudyard Kipling's great "Recessional" of 1897.

> God of our fathers, known of old,
> Lord of our far-flung battle-line,
> Beneath whose awful Hand we hold
> Dominion over palm and pine—
> Lord God of Hosts, be with us yet,
> Lest we forget—lest we forget!

This is precisely what Joshua was saying to the people. It was the God of their fathers who had been with them in battle and had given the dominion they now held. Now Joshua was challenging them to remember this and pray that the Lord of Hosts might be with them yet, lest they forget it.

But it was not only the identity and character of the true God that they were to remember. They were also to remember what they had been and would still be, were it not for God's sovereign choice of them to be his people. God began with Abraham, as we know. Joshua mentions Abraham. But Abraham is not mentioned to remind the people of their supposed illustrious ancestry but rather to remind them of their humble and utterly pagan beginnings. The point is that ". . . long ago your forefathers, including Terah the father of Abraham and Nahor, lived beyond the River and *worshiped other gods*" (Joshua 24:2, emphasis mine).

People have the idea that when God chose Abraham to be the father of the Jewish people, he looked for someone with a little bit of saving faith and when he found such faith in Abraham, he saved Abraham and began the Jewish nation through him. But that is entirely backward. God tells us what he sees when he looks upon the unregenerate heart. Jeremiah quoted God as saying, "The heart is deceitful above all things and beyond cure. Who can understand it?" (Jeremiah 17:9). Moses wrote, "The LORD saw how great man's wickedness on the earth had become, and that every inclination of the thoughts of his heart was only evil all the time" (Genesis 6:5). The apostle Paul declared, "There is no one righteous, not even one; there is no one who understands, no one who seeks God. All have turned away, they have together become worthless; there is no one who does good, not even one" (Romans 3:10–12; *see* Psalms 14:1–3; 53:1–3; Ecclesiastes 7:20).

If that is what the heart of man is like from God's perspective, then how could God possibly look down from heaven and find something good in anyone—unless he had first put it there? How could he find faith in Abraham unless the faith he found was his own prior gift to the patriarch?

That is Joshua's point. In reminding the people of their past, he

was not reminding them of some great heritage they were being
challenged to live up to, but rather of the fact that they had been
pagans, worshipers of false gods, before God called them. They
were to live for him because of who they had been and what he
had done for them.

It is the same for us. Paul says:

> As for you, you were dead in your transgressions and sins,
> in which you used to live when you followed the ways of this
> world and of the ruler of the kingdom of the air, the spirit who
> is now at work in those who are disobedient. All of us also
> lived among them at one time, gratifying the cravings of our
> sinful nature and following its desires and thoughts. Like the
> rest, we were by nature objects of wrath. But because of his
> great love for us, God, who is rich in mercy, made us alive
> with Christ even when we were dead in transgressions—it is by
> grace you have been saved. And God raised us up with Christ
> and seated us with him in the heavenly realms in Christ Jesus,
> in order that in the coming ages he might show the incompa-
> rable riches of his grace, expressed in his kindness to us in
> Christ Jesus. For it is by grace you have been saved, through
> faith—and this not from yourselves, it is the gift of God—not
> by works, so that no one can boast. For we are God's
> workmanship, created in Christ Jesus to do good works, which
> God prepared in advance for us to do.
>
> Ephesians 2:1–10

There is one other point before we move on, and that is the
degree to which our past corruption clings to us, even after many
years of experiencing God's grace. Sometimes when I have
spoken of Israel's pagan ancestry, I have pointed out that in spite
of Abraham's close walk with God and faithful teaching of his
family, idols were still cherished by his family three generations
after God's call to him when he was in pagan Ur. I refer to the
incident regarding Rachel, Jacob's favorite wife, who hid her
father's household gods under a saddle and sat on it when he
searched the camp believing that someone in Jacob's entourage

had stolen them. How horrible! How amazing that these idols were still possessed and cherished even into the third generation of the patriarchs!

But in Joshua 24 we have something more amazing still. Here Joshua urges his people to ". . . throw away the gods your forefathers worshiped beyond the River and in Egypt . . ." and "throw away the foreign gods that are among you . . ." (vv. 14, 23). This is not the third generation after Abraham. There had been scores of generations by this time. Moreover, the years that had passed had been years of the greatest blessing and of great demonstrations of the power of the true God over all the other "gods." Yet even here, at one of the greatest peaks in all Israel's long history, it was necessary for Joshua to urge the destruction of these idols.

Are we better? Those who know their hearts know that the sins of the past cling closely to us and are a danger at every turn. So it is always necessary to reject the false and choose (and continue always to choose) to worship and serve the true God.

Choose This Day

In his study of this chapter, Francis Schaeffer points out rightly that when Joshua challenged the people to choose to serve God and affirmed that this was his settled choice as well, the tense he used implied more than a once-for-all choosing, as if one can make a choice and be done with it thereafter. The tense involves what grammarians call continuous action. That is, it involves the past, but it also involves the present and the future. It is as if Joshua had said, "I have chosen to serve the Lord; I am choosing that same path of service now; and I will go on choosing to serve God until the very end."

Schaeffer writes, "This was the character of Joshua. He chose, and he chose, and he chose, and he kept right on choosing. He understood the dynamics of choice—once-for-all choice and existential choice as well. Thus his word to the people was not an affirmation puffed up on the spur of the moment. It was deeply imbedded in Joshua's comprehension of what is required of a person made in the image of God, one called upon not to obey God like a machine or an animal, but to obey God by choice.''[1]

Joshua did not limit the choices or misrepresent the options when presenting his case to the people, because although God had chosen them, having called Abraham when he was still a worshiper of idols in Ur and having called the entire nation out of Egypt, the people nevertheless had to choose God themselves—intelligently, decisively, and willingly—if their choice was to be of real value. Joshua gave them four options:

1. The gods their forefathers had served while in Ur of the Chaldeans. This is what ''beyond the River'' refers to. The River is the Euphrates, and the gods served beyond the River were the gods of the Babylonian pantheon.

2. The gods served in Egypt. These were quite different gods from those of Babylon. They were the gods of the Nile, the land, and the sky. Ra, the sun god, was the great god of Egypt. He was thought to be continually embodied in the ruling Pharaoh. When God brought the people from Egypt by means of the ten plagues, it was against the gods of the Nile, land, and sky that the plagues were directed. The plagues showed the Egyptian gods to be impotent.

3. The gods of the Amorites, in whose land the Jews were then living. These were horrible gods, like Molech, who demanded the sacrifice of newborn infants. Many of the gods were fertility gods worshiped by cultic prostitution.

4. The true God who had made Israel into a people, had

1. Francis A. Schaeffer, *Joshua and the Flow of Biblical History* (Downers Grove, Ill.: InterVarsity Press, 1975), p. 208.

brought them out of Egypt, and had established them in their own land, a good land, as he had promised.

The Good Fight Ended, the Race Run

What would the people of Israel choose? Verbally the choice was clear. "Far be it from us to forsake the LORD to serve other gods!" they protested. "It was the LORD our God himself who brought us and our forefathers up out of Egypt, from that land of slavery, and performed those great signs before our eyes. He protected us on our entire journey and among all the nations through which we traveled. And the LORD drove out before us all the nations, including the Amorites, who lived in the land. We too will serve the LORD, because he is our God" (vv. 16–18).

True enough! But Joshua seemed to detect a note of insincerity, or at least glibness, in this predictable and ready response. Did he suspect they were taking the whole thing too lightly? Were they supposing they had the power in themselves to serve God, instead of acknowledging that only God himself could keep them faithful?

These must have been Joshua's thoughts, for he replied, "You are not able to serve the LORD. He is a holy God; he is a jealous God. He will not forgive your rebellion and your sins. If you forsake the LORD and serve foreign gods, he will turn and bring disaster on you and make an end of you, after he has been good to you" (vv. 19, 20).

The people were self-confident. "No! We will serve the LORD."

"You are witnesses against yourselves that you have chosen to serve the LORD," said Joshua (v. 22).

"Yes, we are witnesses," they answered.

"Then throw away your foreign gods," said Joshua.

"Oh, yes," they said. "We will serve the LORD our God and obey him" (v. 24).

More words were useless. So Joshua took the affirmation as given, drew up a covenant between the people and God, and recorded the fact that he had done so. The book of Joshua, especially this chapter, is the record. Then he erected a large stone as a memorial and uttered his parting words: " 'See!' he said to all the people. 'This stone will be a witness against us. It has heard all the words the Lord has said to us. It will be a witness against you if you are untrue to your God' " (v. 27). Joshua had fought the good fight. He had finished his race. He had kept the faith. Now there was laid up for him that crown of righteousness that the Lord, the righteous Judge, would award him on that day—and not to him only, but to all who love him and long for his appearing (*see* 2 Timothy 4:7, 8).

What more can any of us do? We cannot make others' choices for them; we cannot guarantee their future. In this case, we are told that "Israel served the Lord throughout the lifetime of Joshua and of the elders who outlived him and who had experienced everything the Lord had done for Israel" (v. 31). But in the very next book of the Bible, in the second chapter where this very verse is repeated, we are told, "After that whole generation had been gathered to their fathers, another generation grew up, who knew neither the Lord nor what he had done for Israel. Then the Israelites did evil in the eyes of the Lord and served the Baals. They forsook the Lord, the God of their fathers, who had brought them out of Egypt. They followed and worshiped various gods of the peoples around them . . ." (Judges 2:10–12).

That may be true in our case, also. A generation from now, those who follow us may utterly forsake the Lord. They may go after the evil gods of our materialistic culture. *But we must not do it!* We must say with Joshua, "But as for me and my household, we will serve the Lord."

Subject Index

189

Scripture Index